Cotton Patch
for the Kingdom

Clarence Jordan's Demonstration
Plot at Koinonia Farm

Ann Louise Coble

Herald
Press

Scottdale, Pennsylvania
Waterloo, Ontario

Library of Congress Cataloging-in-Publication Data
Coble, Ann Louise, 1960-
Cotton path for the Kingdom : Clarence Jordan's demonstration plot
at Koinonia Farm / Ann Louise Coble.
    p. cm.
Includes bibliographical references and index.
ISBN 0-8361-9166-8
1. Koinonia Farm—History. 2. Jordan, Clarence. I. Title.
BV4407.67 .C63 2001
277.58'913—dc21
    2001004815

COTTON PATCH FOR THE KINGDOM
Copyright © 2002 by Herald Press, Scottdale, Pa. 15683
    Published simultaneously in Canada by Herald Press,
    Waterloo, Ont. N2L 6H7. All rights reserved
Library of Congress Catalog Card Number: 2001004815
International Standard Book Number: 0-8361-9166-8
Printed in the United States of America
Book and cover design by Jim Butti
All photos courtesy of Hargrett Rare Book & Manuscript
    Library/University of Georgia Libraries. Reprinted with permission.

10 09 08 07 06 05 04 03 02 01 10 9 8 7 6 5 4 3 2 1

To order or request information, please call 1-800-759-4447 (individuals);
1-800-245-7894 (trade). Website: www.mph.org

Cotton Patch
for the Kingdom

In memory of my father,
Dr. Harold Dwain Coble,
who constantly
encouraged me to think.

Contents

Foreword

Somebody once said that when a student is ready to learn, the teacher appears.

I was ready to learn when my wife, Linda, and I left our life of affluence in Montgomery, Alabama, and showed up on Koinonia's doorstep. Clarence Jordan was there and he became my teacher, my spiritual mentor.

On our first visit to Koinonia, we intended to visit for a couple of hours. We stayed a month. During that time I spent many hours talking to Clarence. I needed guidance at a crucial juncture in my life. He was patient and kind. He helped me in innumerable ways, but especially in getting to know about a Jesus I really had never met, even though I had been raised in the Church. Clarence Jordan, purely and simply, took Jesus seriously. He was seeking to be an authentic disciple. I was deeply touched and forever changed by that special time I got to spend with him.

Clarence thought more like Jesus than anybody I had ever known. He constantly reminded me that Jesus called on us to love our neighbors as we love ourselves, and no one took this biblical teaching more seriously than Clarence. His faith was a living one, full of dynamism and great strength.

How radical is it to ask Christians to live out Jesus' Sermon on the Mount? What does it mean to truly love your neighbors and even your enemies as you love yourself? This was Clarence's vision of the Christian faith. This was his commitment and life's work.

Linda and I left Koinonia after that month's stay. We were occupied with other things until mid-1968 when we returned to the farm to live. I had the joyous experience of working with him on a daily basis until his sudden death on October 29, 1969. During this longer time at Koinonia, I continued to work and dream and plan with Clarence. It was so exhilarating to be with him.

One of the things we talked about was housing for our low-income neighbors. Then, as now, housing was a relevant issue in Americus and Sumter County. Clarence would say, "If your neighbor is living in miserable conditions and you have a decent place to live, you certainly aren't loving your neighbor as yourself. You'd better get busy and help them have a decent place to live." That's just the way he thought! And his thinking impacted mine.

We launched a program called "Partnership Housing." One house was started, but before it could be finished, Clarence died. However, Linda and I and a growing number of others kept the program going in south Georgia. A few years later, Linda and I moved our family to Africa where we launched a program of house building, patterned on the work at Koinonia.

We returned from Africa in 1976 and in an old abandoned chicken barn at Koinonia, had the organizing meeting for Habitat for Humanity. Although long dead, Clarence was surely there in our midst, in spirit. I have always considered him to be the spiritual father of Habitat for Humanity.

As serious as he was about being a disciple of Jesus and about being a vital part of what he called "the God movement," Clarence also had a tremendous sense of humor. When Jesus was confronted with a difficult question, he would often turn the heat back on the questioner. Clarence was like that. One time, when he was finished giving a speech, a man in the audience stood up and said, "Folks, this man is a good talker, but you need to understand, he's a Communist."

Clarence replied, "Sir, why do you say I'm a Communist?"

"Well," he said, "you fraternize with Myles Horton"—a famous white union organizer and civil-rights supporter. The man said, "I've got it on good report that Myles Horton has been down to Koinonia for meetings, and everybody knows Myles Horton is a Communist. Birds of a feather flock together. So, I know you're a Communist."

Clarence shot back, "Well, I'll readily admit that Myles Horton has been to Koinonia. I think he's a fine man, and we've given him hospitality at Koinonia. But, sir, if you showed up at Koinonia, we'd give you hospitality, too. But you know, I really have trouble with your logic. I don't think my talking to Myles Horton makes me a Communist any more than my talking to you right now makes me a jackass."

Koinonia sold pecans and other products on the roadside in Sumter County, and some locals didn't like that, so they burned the stand down one night. Clarence went out there and built it back, and then someone put dynamite in it and blew it up. Koinonia got the message that they weren't going to be selling any more stuff on the roadside. Not to be outdone, Koinonia started selling pecans through the mail with the advertising slogan, created by Clarence, "Help Us Ship the Nuts Out of Georgia."

It was putting this kind of humor and good sense to work that allowed Clarence's Kingdom-building to continue in a very turbulent period in the South's history.

This book gives you an in-depth look and a real understanding of the man, Clarence Jordan and the Koinonia "experiment." You'll be moved by what you read here and, I hope, changed, to be more like Jesus. Clarence would be enormously pleased if you were so changed!

—*Millard Fuller*
Founder & President, Habitat for Humanity International
Americus, Georgia
October 2001

Preface

I was first introduced to the writings of Clarence Jordan when I was in high school. My Young Life leaders had me read Jordan's book *Sermon on the Mount,* and I was immediately drawn in to the kind of faith Jordan described. Jesus, according to Jordan, was calling Christians to be the freest of all people. We could freely love our neighbors, freely give of our time and money, and freely question all of society's constraints. At the same time, Jordan's Jesus was calling Christians to be self-sacrificial and to use this freedom for God's purposes. I was gripped by both the vast horizon that opened to me and the sense of direction in Jordan's vision of the Christian faith.

Later, when I was looking for a dissertation topic, I was given the following advice: "Pick a topic that you can eat and sleep and breathe for three years and that you will continue to enjoy for ten years after that." I took the counsel to heart, and I looked for a subject that would be, not only academically interesting, but also spiritually challenging. Remembering Jordan's unique expression of Christianity, I chose to study him. In doing so, I have a sense that my faith has come full circle from those early years.

I thank Regina Siegfried, Francis Nichols, and particularly my dissertation advisor, James T. Fisher. Each one assisted me in the research and writing process in different ways, and I appreciate all of their guidance and assistance.

I also thank the librarians at the Hargrett Rare Books and Manuscript Library at the University of Georgia Libraries, Athens, Georgia.

I am grateful to Neb Hayden, who first introduced me to Clarence Jordan's writings and to Roger Steffen, in memoriam, whose love of Jesus and the Cotton Patch versions continues to inspire me. I thought then, as I think now, that this is true religion.

Most of all, I am particularly grateful to my mother, Harriet Ann Coble, who encouraged me to keep going and who lovingly and carefully edited an earlier draft of this book.

— Ann Louise Coble
Westminster College
February 2001

Cotton Patch
for the Kingdom

1

A Demonstration Plot

The setting is Louisville, Kentucky, in the late 1930s, and racial tensions are at a peak. A group of angry black men has assembled in a small room to plan retaliation for an incidence of violence. These men know that some white men in the community are guilty of violent acts. Voices grow louder as the men, who are obviously the recipients of years of injustice, are seeking retribution, an eye for an eye. One man swings a section of iron pipe and declares, "Just like the whites kill a Negro for this, I'm going to kill a white man."

As the crowd is at the point of taking up weapons, the only white man at the meeting steps forward and says, "If a white man must die for this, . . . let it be me. Do it now." Clarence Jordan's words shock these men, many of them his friends, into silence. The crowd looks at the situation through new eyes, and after some discussion they work for a different response to this injustice.[1]

Who was this man Clarence Jordan? What made him work for racial reconciliation in the South? In the face of repeated incidents of racial violence, what made him choose peaceful means to fight racial hatred? Clarence Jordan was an ordinary, Southern Baptist good old boy who was willing to take a peaceful stand against racial violence from both sides. Why? He chose to stand against racial injustice—and to use nonviolent means—because of his commitment to living out his understanding of Jesus' Sermon on the Mount.

In 1942, Clarence and Florence Jordan and Martin and Mabel England moved to a small farm in Sumter County, Georgia, and started an agriculture-based religious community. Clarence, who had a Ph.D. in Greek New Testament, named it "Koinonia Farm." *Koinonia*, as it is used in the New Testament, is a rich word that includes the ideas of fellowship, community, sharing, generosity, and close relationships.[2] The Englands soon left to return to their missionary work, but within the first ten years, a few new families moved into the community. Clarence Jordan, a Baptist minister, functioned as the unofficial leader.

During that time, Jordan focused on applying new techniques in agriculture and teaching them to the nearby farmers and sharecroppers. Like many similar communities, Koinonia Farm members held their finances in common. Unlike many similar communities, Koinonia Farm was not intended to be a separatist endeavor; farm members were active in the local community, attended the local churches, and sold their crops at the local grain elevator and at a neighborhood roadside market.

Jordan had seen some of the effects of racism during his early life in rural Georgia and during his time at Southern Baptist Theological Seminary in Louisville, Kentucky. However, it was at Koinonia Farm that Jordan took a series of small but significant stands against the racist practices around him. In the early years, all the members of Koinonia Farm were white, educated, and middle-class. Some of the local people hired to help with the farming were white and some black, and it was there that Jordan began anti-racist practices such as having all the workers, black and white, eat the noon meal together and paying all the workers the same wages.

In addition, Jordan's pacifism and preaching of nonviolence, together with the common ownership of property and income, led the people of Sumter County to suspect Koinonia Farm of anti-American and Communist activities. Throughout the 1950s and early 1960s, Koinonia Farm endured persecution. There were repeated acts of violence by the Ku Klux Klan, resulting in injuries for a few Koinonia members and the bombing of a roadside market. The Sumter County judicial system viewed Koinonia with distrust, fearing the group was pro-Communist, and the farm members were blamed for inciting the violent acts.

Meanwhile, local feed stores refused to sell fertilizer or seed to Jordan or other members, and the local grain elevators boycotted Koinonia Farm produce. To offset that, Koinonia members began their own mail-order business, which remains the chief source of farm income today. Eventually the local Baptist church forced the Jordans and other members of the Koinonia community to leave on the grounds that they were allowing the races to mix.

From the mid-1950s until 1969, Jordan worked on his Cotton Patch versions of the New Testament. They were loose paraphrases of the books of the New Testament, rewritten so that the setting for the events in Jesus' life was twentieth-century Georgia and the main tension was between blacks and whites. He traveled throughout the United States, preaching mostly from the New Testament and speaking about ways to fight racism.

While remaining numerically small, Koinonia Farm became well known in Baptist circles, among the rising Christian counter-culture, and among a slice of both the progressive and the conservative churches that were interested in community life and in fighting racism. As a result, Jordan became a public figure and Koinonia Farm a model of resistance to racial persecution for a diverse cross-section of American Christianity.

What was Jordan trying to do when he established Koinonia Farm? Because of the focus in the media on racial issues, many have assumed that Jordan had intended primarily to establish an interracial community and that his Christian faith was of secondary importance—or perhaps of no real importance—in the establishment of Koinonia Farm. Racial tension had certainly come to the fore in the media. Some, largely Jordan's opponents, believed he had begun Koinonia Farm for the purpose of establishing a beachhead for Communism in the United States. Jordan's pacifism and insistence on joint ownership of property by Koinonia members contributed to that mistaken view.

However, I would argue that Clarence Jordan was trying to flesh out his understanding of primitive Christianity by making Koinonia Farm what he called "a demonstration plot for the kingdom of God."[3] Jordan was captured by a vision of the kingdom of God, and it was because of that vision that he fought racism, helped develop and teach new agricultural techniques, and fought poverty. It was because of his conception of what the kingdom might look like if it were lived out that he began a community based on nonviolence and the radical sharing of property and income.

Jordan's love of the Jesus of the Gospels led him to attempt an incarnate interpretation of the New Testament in the form of Koinonia Farm. He frequently used the term *incarnate* to mean "lived-out in every area of life," and Koinonia was to be the place where his interpretation of the kingdom might be put into practice.[4] Jordan's agricultural experiment was theologically—rather than sociologically, politically, or philosophically—driven.

This is not a theological book but rather a history of Jordan and Koinonia Farm that places Jordan's theology at the center. The biographical information about Jordan and historical information about Koinonia Farm is based on published sources and archival materials. I am indebted to Tracy K'Meyer's excellent history of Koinonia Farm.[5]

Jordan was a natural storyteller, and I have included many of the stories that he recounted in his written works and sermons to illustrate his motivation in creating the community.[6] It is through these stories that Jordan's concern with the biblical text, particularly the Sermon on the Mount,[7] becomes evident as his foundation for racial reconciliation, communal living, and pacifism.

As I seek to answer the question of why Jordan established Koinonia Farm, I will look at the thinking expressed through his writings and taped lectures and sermons. Jordan was noted for his paraphrases of the Gospels and other books of the New Testament. These versions, commonly known as the Cotton Patch versions, provide a rich resource for understanding Jordan's slant on Christianity. In these texts he interprets the New Testament in light of the social and political situations of the 1950s and 1960s in Georgia.

Before writing the Cotton Patch Versions, Jordan wrote a book on Jesus' Sermon on the Mount, a key text in the community's formation. This book gives us much of Jordan's original vision for community, and it lends significant support to the argument presented here.[8] A chapter of this work is devoted to Jordan's *Sermon on the Mount* along with some of his early sermons.

Jordan preached often, and many of his sermons are preserved either on cassette tapes (originally on reel-to-reel) or as written texts. This is a unique series of work because it shows the changing emphases in his thinking throughout his ministry. The sermons are also important because in these we see Jordan's application of biblical texts for particular congregations at specific moments in time.

The second chapter describes Clarence Jordan's life before he enrolled in Southern Baptist Theological Seminary. The purpose of this chapter is to provide a background of Jordan's early life, including some indications of his family life; his experiences with church, race relations, and the Reserve Officer Training Corps (ROTC); and his training in agriculture.

In the third chapter, I describe Jordan's training at Southern Baptist Theological Seminary in Louisville, Kentucky, along with some significant background information about the churches of the Southern Baptist Convention. I focus on Jordan's New Testament training and his love of New Testament Greek. Jordan's involvement with the local mission to African-Americans is explored, as well as his efforts to fight the racism he saw at the seminary.

In chapter 4, I explain the details of Jordan's idea for Koinonia Farm and how it came into being. This includes the Jordans' relationship with the Englands, the other founding couple; the details of how they chose to become a rural community; and how they picked the location for Koinonia Farm.

Chapter 5 describes the early years at Koinonia Farm, with an emphasis on Jordan's interest in new, more effective agricultural techniques. From 1942 to 1949, Jordan spent much of his time helping the local farmers learn how to farm more productively, and that led to increased interaction with local African-American farmers and sharecroppers. The racial attitudes and practices of the time in southern Georgia are explored, as well as Jordan's early methods of fighting racism.

In chapter 6, I focus on the 1950s. That decade was a turbulent and confusing time for Koinonia Farm. During the 1950s, Clarence Jordan stood up for his beliefs in ways that directly confronted southern culture. Sumter County residents responded with open hatred, rejection, and violence. Koinonia members, in turn, responded with nonviolence, charity, and steadfastness.

Chapter 7 continues the discussion on the 1950s, but it describes Jordan's writing and preaching during that time. His theological development and its impact both within the Koinonia community and on individuals and groups outside Koinonia are explored. Jordan's book *Sermon on the Mount* is looked at in detail, as well as a selection of his sermons.

In chapter 8, I explore the 1960s, more difficult times for Koinonia Farm. I show how members of the farm responded to the civil rights movement and how the American hippie movement and its expression among Christians impacted life at Koinonia Farm.

Chapter 9 analyzes Jordan's Cotton Patch New Testament with attention to the ways Jordan understood the kingdom of God. In these Cotton Patch books Jordan most clearly puts forth his understanding of Christianity. Koinonia Farm members lived out that vision of the Christian faith as an incarnate interpretation of the New Testament.

Chapter 10, an epilogue, begins with the death of Clarence Jordan in 1969. It then provides a description of the people and events that shaped Koinonia Farm after Jordan's death; these include the reorganization of Koinonia Farm into Koinonia Partners, the founding of the Fund for Humanity and Habitat for Humanity, and the offshoot groups Jubilee Partners and Hope House.

2

Clarence Jordan's Early Years

In the early years of the twentieth century, farming formed the basis of the economy in the American South, the Southern Baptist church was a dominant social force, and the gap between blacks and whites was never more evident than on Sunday morning. After the end of the Civil War, African-American churches developed separately from white congregations.[1] Because black Christians were not given opportunities for leadership in the existing white churches, they began separate black Protestant denominations.

Katherine Dvorak, writing about this phenomenon, states that "by 1871 the pattern of joint worship that prevailed throughout the antebellum period had changed to one of virtually total racial separation."[2] The segregation of the churches mirrored the segregation of southern society. The separation of the Baptist churches was particularly important in southern culture, as historian Paul Harvey points out:

White and black Baptists profoundly influenced each other. Together, and separately, they created different but intertwined southern cultures that shaped Baptists in deep and lasting ways.[3]

The impact of the Baptist church was not limited to Sunday morning. The individualism and autonomy that characterized church life also influenced the southern way of life in general. As Harvey notes, "The congregational-ism of Baptist church governance also continued to shape the lives of southern believers and the larger culture."[4] Historian Nathan Hatch has argued that the concept of democracy greatly influenced religious life in the United States; this is seen quite clearly in the Baptist churches of the South in the early part of the twentieth century.[5]

Autonomy fueled by democratic ideals presented a fertile field for Jordan's independent theology to flourish. It also undermined the older sense of community, which created an opening for his vision of communal living. Although Jordan was rejected by his southern neighbors and expelled from the local Southern Baptist church, his ideas were able to grow because of the independent southern culture. To understand Jordan in his setting, let us begin with his early family life.

Childhood

It was July 1912, and the setting was the rural Georgia town of Talbotton. The area was poor, the land over-farmed, and the people divided: black and white. Clarence Leonard Jordan was born that summer, the sev-enth of ten children born to J. W. and Maude Josey Jordan.[6] Of the seven who survived infancy, Clarence was in the middle. J. W. Jordan was the founder of the Bank of Talbotton and a businessman, and, while still middle-class, it put his family well above most of the people in town.[7] With the help of Clarence and his brothers, Mr. Jordan also ran a general store.[8]

Clarence had a good childhood, pleasant and in many ways uneventful. His great love and respect for his parents is demonstrated in the dedication of his doctoral dissertation: "To my Dad, in humble appreciation of his unfailing love and sacrifice; and to the memory of my Mother, in gratitude for the challenge of her noble and saintly life, I dedicate this volume."[9] Clarence was close to his mother, as is shown in his faithful correspondence during college and seminary, until Mrs. Jordan's death in 1935.[10] Once, when he had forgotten to send a card for Mother's Day, Clarence even sent a telegram to his mother.[11] He was her favorite child, but Florence Jordan made a point of stating that it did not lead the other children to jealousy.[12]

The Jordans were devout Christians, active in the local Baptist church. They regularly attended services and Sunday school, and they had family devotional times of reading the Bible and praying. Clarence was ten when he attended a revival meeting that led to his personal affirmation of faith; he subsequently joined the church.[13] Clarence's five brothers and one sister all made professions of faith and joined the church when they were about twelve years old.[14]

Unlike his brothers and sister, Clarence liked to be alone. He spent time listening to his mother tell stories of her childhood while the other children were playing. He was sensitive and kind, and he took life seriously. As Dallas Lee points out, he taught himself to type and play the piano and was considered the shy and quiet one. He was involved in sports and other school activities, but he had to work hard, because they did not come naturally to him.[15] His character revealed determination: he was not afraid to take on a difficult job and pursue it to the end. He would need that perseverance later in life.

While not excelling in sports, Clarence began to excel

in verbal and written skills. Clarence was known as a verbal fighter in his family. He would argue with any of his siblings, older or younger, as well as his parents. His ability to argue a point, along with his determination to see an argument through, led his family to assume he would become a lawyer. It also led to his nickname, *Grump*. Clarence was not offended by the nickname, sometimes using it to sign his schoolwork.[16]

Clarence's siblings considered him unique. His oldest brother, Frank, said of him, "He always was a little different, saw things differently than we did."[17] Tracy K'Meyer speculates that this might be the result of a childhood bout of scarlet fever, when Clarence spent an extended period of time with only his mother and an African-American nurse.[18] A different approach came through in his intellect, his earnest faith, and his early questioning of race relations. He did very well academically, beginning with grade school and continuing all the way through his seminary Ph.D.[19] He seems to have taken seriously his brother Buddie's admonition: "Let your motto be to take the name of Jordan just a little bit higher than either one of us took it."[20]

The Jordan family had a typical relationship with the black community around them. As a middle-class family, they were in a position of power rather than competition. Frank, George, and Lillian Jordan commented: "We were very close to all the blacks, had friends in the black community, had a black nurse and servants."[21] African-Americans were treated as the subservient *other*. As K'Meyer notes, there was interaction between blacks and whites in rural Georgia, but the role of blacks in that society was strictly defined, and the Jordan family did not challenge these racial roles.[22]

Clarence, however, began to wrestle with the issues of race and religion. He took his faith very seriously, and his own reflections on his childhood bring this out. While a child, he learned the familiar children's song "Jesus Loves the Little Children." The words are:

Jesus loves the little children,
All the children of the world.
Red and yellow, black and white,
They are precious in his sight
Jesus loves the little children of the world.

In his personal journal in graduate school, Clarence reflected on his experience of singing this song as a child:

The question arose in my mind, "Were the little black children precious in God's sight just like the little white children?" The song said they were. Then why were they always so ragged, so dirty and hungry? Did God have favorite children?

I could not figure out the answers to these puzzling questions, but I knew something was wrong. A little light came when I began to realize that perhaps it wasn't God's doings, but man's. God didn't turn them away from our churches—we did. God didn't pay them low wages—we did. God didn't make them live in another section of town and in miserable huts—we did. God didn't make ragged, hungry little boys pick rotten oranges and fruit out of the garbage can and eat them— we did. Maybe they were just as precious in God's sight, but were they precious in ours? My environment told me that they were not very precious in anybody's sight. A nigger was a nigger and must be kept in his place—the place of servitude and inferiority.[23]

As Dallas Lee comments, Jordan's memory probably added quite a bit to his childhood thoughts, but it is clear that Clarence was beginning to question the discontinuity between what he was being taught in church and what he was experiencing in the streets.[24]

Jordan's own record of childhood includes two stories that show him wrestling with the racism he saw around him. When he was about nine or ten, Clarence witnessed an incident in which his father rebuked an African-American man for delivering clothes from the dry cleaners to the front door of their home. Clarence was so embarrassed and angry, even at a young age, that he lectured his father for treating the deliveryman badly.[25]

The second and more significant story that Jordan told about his childhood concerned the Talbot County jail, which was about a hundred yards behind the Jordan home. Chain gangs of prisoners were kept camped outside in the yard of the jailhouse. Clarence was fascinated by the prisoners, and he began cutting through near the camp after school. He made friends with the cook, who often gave him a piece of cornbread, and he struck up conversations with a number of prisoners. Clarence also became familiar with the ways the prisoners were tortured and punished.

Most of the chain gang prisoners were African-Americans who were bound with ankle fetters and short chains between their ankles to keep them from fleeing. Clarence saw that dehumanizing treatment, along with men being bolted into primitive pillories, beaten with whips, and put on a torture-like stretcher. Clarence could hear the noises from the chain gang in his home during the summer when the windows were kept open. He remembered:

> This made tremendous, traumatic impressions on me. It hit me the hardest a night or two after I joined the church during the August revival. I remember it was hot, and I

remember that the warden of the chain gang was singing bass in the choir. I'll never forget how carried away he got singing "Love Lifted Me" that night.

But the next night I was awakened by agonizing groans from the direction of the chain gang camp. I was sure I could recognize who it was, and I was sure I knew what was happening. Ed Russell was in the stretcher. I knew not only who was in the stretcher, I knew who was pulling the rope. The same man who only hours before was so carried away singing "Love Lifted Me" was now lifting that man's body on the stretcher. That nearly tore me to pieces. I identified totally with that man in the stretcher. His agony was my agony. I got really mad with God. If He was love and the warden was an example of it, I didn't want anything to do with Him.[26]

Clarence did not reject God or Christianity, but he realized that the people around him who claimed to be religious were not living the religion he had read about in the New Testament. As Dallas Lee comments, Clarence at age twelve did not immediately begin speaking out against the racism he saw around him; rather, those difficult experiences shaped the part of his character "where conviction slowly matures to action."[27]

Given his natural ability to argue and his family's hopes that he would become a lawyer, Jordan considered going into law. He envisioned himself "raging back into the county like a savior to see that justice was done in the county jails and work camps."[28] That dream was brief, however, as Clarence's vision widened and he saw that the injustices of racism and poverty pervaded the South. "I realized," he remembers, "that most people are not stretched by ropes but by hunger, by oppression."[29]

Clarence turned away from law and politics to take a hard look at the system of sharecropping that was slowly strangling the African-American population. Toward the end of his years in high school, he decided to study scientific agriculture, with the hope of helping poor farmers greatly increase their farming abilities. Looking back on that decision, Clarence said he was increasingly disillusioned by the affluent, racist preachers who ought to change their message from "hellfire and brimstone to phosphate and limestone," referring to the fertilizers needed to replenish the farmland.[30] When he graduated from Talbotton High School on June 3, 1929, Clarence was prepared to pursue scientific farming.[31]

College

In the fall of 1929, Clarence enrolled in the Georgia State College of Agriculture at the University of Georgia in Athens. His family still hoped he would pursue law, and his father commented, "If you want to be a farmer, why go to school? I'll buy you a mule, and you can start right now."[32] However, Mr. Jordan did not seem to disapprove completely. He gave Clarence a checkbook and told him not to worry about money; he supported Clarence until his bank folded under the weight of the Depression in 1933.[33]

Clarence bloomed in college, doing well in his classes as well as participating in a number of campus and church activities. He was in a fraternity, the campus literary society, the debate team, the band, the drama club, the YMCA, and the agricultural honor society.[34] In a letter home in March 1930, he mentioned that his side had won the Freshman Debate and that he was honored to wear the 'gold key.'[35] He was finding his voice as a writer as well as debater, and he wrote for and edited the *Georgia Agriculturalist*.[36]

From his first week at college, Jordan was involved with both the Baptist Student Union and the local Baptist church. He had been raised in the Baptist church and was continuing to develop a spirituality that was distinctly Baptist. He expressed ownership of the faith of his childhood in a letter to his mother written soon after arriving at college: "Since God has blest me with such wonderful parents, certainly I can honor him and keep his word."[37] By his junior year, Jordan was president of his local chapter of the Baptist Student Union of Georgia.[38]

The Southern Baptist Church, in addition to holding to the historic Christian faith, held three doctrinal positions that created a distinctly Baptist ethos. The first was a strong emphasis on the Reformation doctrine of the priesthood of all believers. The effect of that doctrine was to replace the centrality of the church with an emphasis on the faith of the individual. Second was the doctrine of the authority of Scripture. Combined with an individualized spirituality, that meant Baptists centered their faith on their own personal readings of Scripture. The third doctrine was a belief in baptizing after an individual had made a profession of faith. That element of personal choice as a key ingredient of Baptist faith further reinforced an individualized spirituality.

The result was that, as Jordan became more serious about his faith, he focused on personal Bible study and prayer, and he continued to question established societal and church norms around him, using the biblical texts as his standard.

Jordan was very involved with the Baptist Student Union. He led Bible studies and traveled to student retreats and conferences. He also engaged in long discussions about Scripture with his close friend D. B. Nicholson, who was the state and local Baptist Student Union director. Those activities reinforced his focus on the New Testament, and particularly on the Gospels.

During his college years, Jordan also participated in

the Reserve Officers Training Corps (ROTC). In the ROTC he made his first significant break with southern society. In 1932, a professor recommended him for a military summer course that would lead to a commission as a second lieutenant. Jordan attended the summer boot camp course in 1933, and there he began to question his earlier views on the military.[39]

Dallas Lee has pointed out that an officer's position in the U. S. Cavalry was a dream of many southern gentlemen. "Now Clarence Jordan mounted on a bold black steed, a pistol in one hand and a saber in the other, was the fulfillment of a mysterious compulsion common to most sons of southern aristocracy."[40] Jordan had returned to Talbotton for the vacation, proudly showing his boots and spurs.[41] He was moving toward the life of a successful southern aristocrat, but he was beginning to question that dream.

Jordan spent his free time at cavalry boot camp absorbing Jesus' words in the Sermon on the Mount. As he considered his training, he came to the decision that the teachings of the Sermon were in conflict with his boot camp experience. One day he was memorizing Matthew 5:43: "You have heard that it was said, 'You shall love your neighbor and hate your enemy.' But I say to you, Love your enemies."[42] Later that day, Jordan and his cavalry group were engaged in maneuvers in which they charged through a wooded area, shooting or hacking a series of dummies that were set up for the drill. Jordan later recalled:

> Soon I spotted a target. Drawing a bead, I pressed the trigger of my pistol . . . a tiny white spot appeared in the black circle of the dummy's head.
> "But I say to you, LOVE YOUR ENEMIES."
> But he's not my enemy, he's only a dummy. Besides,

I'm just practicing. Well, someday it will be a real man, but after all one must be prepared to defend himself.

"But I say to you, love your ENEMIES."

Another dummy. I was well past it before I saw it, and my hand was trembling. When I arrived on the other side there was only one empty cartridge in my pistol. It was crystal clear that this Jesus was going one way and I another. Yet I called myself his follower.[43]

Moments later, as Jordan came out of the woods, he dismounted, approached his commanding officer, and resigned his commission. During that conversation, the officer suggested that he might become a chaplain. Jordan remembers, "I told him that that would be worse than ever. I could not encourage someone else to do what I myself would not do."[44] Eventually that same officer told him, "Son, I hope someday you make my job impossible."[45] From that day onward, Jordan was a confirmed pacifist: he advocated nonviolent solutions to problems, and he would not support any preparations for war.

He returned to Athens, Georgia, and asked the First Baptist Church to license him to preach, which it did. He gained some experience guest preaching at local churches in the Athens area.[46] Jordan was at a point of decision concerning his career; he had almost finished his degree and was trying to decide what to do next. Looking back on his choices, he said he realized that real answers to the problems he saw around him were not economic answers but spiritual ones. "I was driven in a desperate search for spiritual resources," he said.[47] Jordan traveled to a Baptist student retreat in Ridgecrest, North Carolina; there he decided that God's will was for him to be a preacher. Jordan detailed some of his thoughts on being called to the ministry, and he read this statement to the congregation of the First Baptist Church:

If, according to popular opinion, being called to the ministry means spending all night in prayer, fighting constantly that voice which persistently speaks, being borne on the floods of passion, or having an "experience"—I repeat myself—if it means all that, I doubt very much that I have been called. But if being called to the ministry means lending an attentive ear to a simple statement, "My child, I want you to preach for me," then most assuredly I have been called to the ministry.

While I admit that God may choose the former method of speaking to those whom he wishes to preach, nevertheless I contend that it is not necessary, nor is it the only method. Behold a tree. Does it not speak to us thusly: "Don't you see that God is not working Himself into a frenzy in me? I am calmly, quietly, silently pouring forth my life and bringing forth fruit. Do thou likewise."

And so it was with me. No battle was fought. My heart and soul were not torn by doubt, for when His voice came I was sure of its source. My strength was never pitted against His. He spoke. I listened. I can still hear him just as vividly: "My child, I want you to preach for me." You wish my answer? Here it is: "Yes, Lord, whatever you say, just promise me that you'll go with me." "And lo, I am with thee alway, even unto the end of the world." "Lead on, O Christ, I'll follow." And that's all there was to it.[48]

Clarence did not consider his call to ministry to be in conflict with or to supersede his interest and training in agriculture. He was beginning to consider the possibility of attending seminary, and he hoped to combine preaching with helping the poor. He put that idea into practice during seminary, and it eventually led to the founding of Koinonia Farm.

❋   ❋   ❋

Jordan attributes the decision to study agriculture, the decision to leave the ROTC, and the decision to pursue the pastorate to his increasing commitment to follow the Jesus he had come to know in the Gospels. Baptist spirituality, focused on an individualized faith and centered on a personal reading of the Bible, helped lead him into biblical studies at seminary. Dallas Lee states that Jordan finished college with two convictions pushing him forward: the conviction to not participate in oppression of blacks and the conviction to be a pacifist.[49] Those may indeed have shaped Jordan's future, but it was his continuing saturation in the Scriptures and his desire to alter his life to follow the biblical models that enabled Jordan to stand by those positions.

3

The Seminary Years

Clarence Jordan began studying for a master of divinity degree in the fall of 1933 at Southern Baptist Theological Seminary in Louisville, Kentucky; he stayed for six years, completing a Ph.D. in Greek New Testament. That seminary was the most prestigious Southern Baptist institution at the time, considered "the matriarch of Southern Baptist seminaries."[1] At first Jordan felt out of place, living so much farther north than he had thus far in a city much larger than Talbotton. He kept a journal in which he wrote: "At first I mistook the students for professors. Everyone looked so distinguished I thought surely he must be a prof."[2]

Jordan jumped into language studies wholeheartedly. He excelled in both Greek and Hebrew, finishing his Hebrew studies with a 98.8 average.[3] He did well in all his courses, developing a particular love for New Testament Greek. When Jordan later reflected on his time learning under Southern Baptist scholars A. T. Robertson, Hersey Davis, and J. B. Weatherspoon, he commented, "They didn't teach me *about* the Bible, they taught me the Bible."[4]

Jordan saw his study of the biblical texts to be crucial in his preparation for working in rural Georgia. He wanted to read the Scriptures in the original languages and to be able to argue his points against both laity and clergy. "I didn't want some little jackleg preacher tying me up in knots because I didn't know what my Lord said," he explained, "and I rooted myself in the Greek language that I might understand."[5] That was Jordan's desire and goal: to understand what his Lord had said.

With regard to the state of biblical studies in the Southern Baptist Convention, and particularly at Southern Baptist Theological Seminary, some believe that the conservative concepts regarding the Bible taught by his professors negatively influenced Jordan by limiting his uses of Scripture.[6] However, the professors at Southern were not constrictingly conservative. They actually stood at the moderate end of the Southern Baptist church and were teaching the basics of higher criticism.[7]

Jordan's own view of the Bible was more conservative than that of his professors, and he was sometimes suspicious of them. He commented to his friend Henlee Barnette that he "learned a lot of New Testament Greek in spite of" his teachers.[8] In addition, it was precisely Jordan's grasp of Scripture and his dedication to living it out that led him into an unconventional life.

Barnette states that Jordan's professors at Southern taught him critical methods and the social gospel, and that their teaching provided the basis for his views on social and racial issues.[9] Barnette's book accurately portrays the professors at Southern, but does not give an authentic account of Jordan's theology.

Jordan's approach to biblical interpretation indicates very little influence of higher criticism, and he treated the Bible in an almost literal way. His books and collections of sermons do not reflect a questioning of Scripture, but a drivenness to live it out. It is easy to make the mistake of assuming that progressive views of Scripture must go hand in hand with more progressive social stances. In Jordan's case, he was inconsistent in his use of higher criticism, but he generally held to a conservative view of the Bible. It is precisely in taking the Bible literally that Jordan drew out radical views of social issues, particularly that of racial justice.

One of the most influential professors Jordan studied under was Edward A. McDowell Jr.[10] McDowell encouraged Jordan to steep himself in Greek in order better to understand the Word of God; that "the Word must come alive in currents of history and social change."[11] In the mid-1930s, McDowell took a group of students to a meeting of the Southern Interracial Commission. Jordan was among them, and in a letter he wrote to McDowell: "This too was a turning point in my life, for it seemed to bring into the open the deep feelings which had lain, like molten lava, within the inner recesses of my heart."[12]

Jordan was active in a variety of ministries throughout his time at seminary. He developed his skills as a preacher, soon becoming a popular supply preacher and often spending his Sundays traveling to small congregations in Kentucky and southern Indiana. Those guest-preaching engagements led to a series of pastorates with smaller churches. During his time at seminary, Jordan pastored Knob Hill Church, Mt. Carmel Church, and Vine Hill Church, all in the Louisville area, and the Baptist Church in Clermont, Kentucky. As Joel Snider notes, those seminary pastorates were the only ones Jordan ever held.[13]

The large number of poor people from rural areas coming to Louisville hoping to find work or food during the Depression years overwhelmed Jordan. Soon after arriving in Louisville, he wrote to his mother of the heartbreaking conditions of the people and his desire to minister "in the service of suffering humanity."[14] Through his first three years in seminary, although he did not act until later, he felt keenly the needs of the poor in Louisville.

In Jordan's second year at Southern, his mother

became gravely ill. Living away from home, Clarence was not aware of his mother's serious condition until he received a telegram from his father on January 19, 1935. [15] Clarence, as already noted, was the child closest to Maude Jordan, and he was quite traumatized by her illness and subsequent death.

Florence

While Clarence spent long hours studying in the library, it seems he also spent some of the time with the assistant librarian. He admitted he had often checked out books just as an excuse to talk to Florence Kroeger, who was working at the circulation desk. Florence was tall and blonde with beautiful blue eyes, and Clarence was smitten.[16] Finally, he decided to ask her out, and they found they were "a perfect match."[17]

Florence was the daughter of a German immigrant father and a German-American mother who had encouraged her to become a Baptist. James McClendon saw Florence as "free enough from the Kentucky culture to encourage Clarence's own independence of thought and action."[18] Dallas Lee, who was a friend of Florence's, described her as "a strong woman who was quick to air her own opinions but solid in her willingness to do anything she could to give reality to Clarence's increasingly radical views."[19]

Florence was inspired by Clarence's vision of reaching out to the African-American community, and Clarence was encouraged by Florence's sense of adventure.[20] Seminary friend Peyton Thurman commented that Florence "always carried her head just a little higher and had just a little more substance than other girls."[21] In the spring of 1936, Clarence Jordan proposed to Florence, and she happily accepted. He told Florence that he would not be taking a large church, but he wanted to return to the South and work with poor people in rural areas. Florence was in full agreement with his vision, and she was particularly supportive of his views on racial equality.[22] Clarence's father wrote this letter to him, about a year after the death of his own wife:

> Now that you have made up your mind to marry, I want to tell you that a good woman is one of God's greatest gifts to man, to the world, and to mankind. No man or woman who does not know and love God can truly love one another. God's love is the basis of all happiness and will endure through all time. Since you both love him I know you will love each other and be supremely happy. I know she is a fine woman, and I shall look forward with pleasure to the time when I shall know her. I shall love her doubly, because you love her and because she loves Christ.[23]

Clarence and Florence were married in July 1936, two months after he had received his master of divinity degree. The wedding took place at Florence's parents' home, with Thomas A. Johnson, librarian at Southern Seminary, officiating. With Florence's support, Clarence decided to stay at Southern to pursue a doctorate in Greek New Testament. Remembering that decision, Clarence later commented, "I wanted to root myself firmly in the teachings of Jesus, in the Greek New Testament, to get it fresh from the stream."[24] Clarence was following McDowell's teaching to look for the meaning behind the words. That meant leaving the English translations behind and reading Scripture in its original languages. Because of his interest in the teachings of Jesus, Clarence focused on biblical Greek.

Up to that point, Jordan had had few opportunities to put any of his beliefs about race relations into practice.

Most of his preaching and ministry positions had been with white rural churches. However, he had preached on occasion in hospitals and orphanages in Louisville and had seen shocking poverty there. He had written to his mother about one mission where the congregation was "a handful of ragged, dirty, hungry, and yes, starving humanity."[25]

Beginning in 1936, Clarence Jordan became more regularly involved in the inner-city ministries of Louisville. His graduate fellowship included teaching part-time at Simmons University, a small seminary that trained African-American preachers.[26] Jordan was struck by the fact that most of the students were working full-time while attempting to attend classes and keep up with homework. He could see that racial differences were hurting the black churches, not only economically, but also spiritually. Pastors with good hearts and determination had neither the time nor the money to learn the basics of biblical exegesis, nor were students at Simmons expected to learn the biblical languages; Jordan could see the effects on the state of African-American theological education.

Jordan made friends with some of the Simmons students and tried to involve them in student life at Southern Seminary as much as possible.[27] Once a group of students from Simmons was asked by the student prayer committee to lead the weekly prayer meeting at Mullins Hall on the Southern campus. Jordan also asked the speakers to supper in the dormitory, an invitation normally extended to prayer meeting speakers.

A few days before the event was to take place, the committee informed Clarence that seminary officials, particularly Mr. Bullard—the business manager and Florence's new boss—were opposed to "the Negroes eating in the dining hall."[28] To keep the guest speakers from embarrassment or a painful experience, Clarence and Florence decided to invite them to their own home for dinner. The Southern students heard about that development and a handful of them confronted the seminary president, demanding an explanation for the school's "unchristian conduct."[29] The president backed down from his original decision and invited the guest speakers and the Jordans to dine in the dormitory on the evening of the prayer meeting.

The Long Run Baptist Association

Clarence's final year of his Ph.D. work was quite demanding, and his first child, Eleanor, had been born in the previous May, so he decided to give up his part-time pastorate at Clermont, Kentucky, to concentrate on school and home life. However, soon after the fall term began, the committee of the Long Run Baptist Association of Southern Baptist Churches in metropolitan Louisville asked Clarence to take over the Sunshine Center mission. The mission was located in a slum area in the predominantly black West End. Clarence accepted the position and began in January 1939.[30]

As soon as Jordan became director of the mission, he changed its name from the Sunshine Center to the Baptist Fellowship Center, in an effort to get away from patronizing connotations.[31] When he graduated in May 1939, he became the Long Run Association's first full-time director of missions.[32] Jordan recruited students from Southern Seminary to help him, and he set up a program of outreach into the neighborhood using films, choirs, and preachers from neighborhood churches.[33] Through his work in the West End, Jordan discovered that many of the poor and destitute were rural families who had moved from Alabama and Georgia, hoping to find work.

Jordan wanted the oversight of the mission to be

shared by both white and black groups, so he organized a joint governing committee that consisted of the Long Run Association's Committee on Negro Work and a parallel group appointed by the Louisville Ministers and Deacons Meeting.[34] His goal was to make black churches, rather than missions led by whites, the centers of ministry in black communities.[35] To further the goal, Jordan set up a library for "colored pastors," requested Bibles from local churches and mission groups, and set up pastor training centers in five local black churches.[36] The Baptist Fellowship Center offered summer classes in Old Testament for black pastors and a training program for black Sunday school teachers and youth workers.[37] The Center also sponsored vacation Bible schools with 1,200 students and summer camp for black girls.[38]

In addition, Jordan wanted to provide opportunities for black and white church leaders to enter into fellowship and learn from each other. He set up combined ministerial meetings and deacons' meetings, which faced antagonism from some white pastors in Louisville. W. C. Boone, pastor of Crescent Hill Church, was one of the most outspoken. Boone was appalled that Jordan not only ate meals with black people, but also planned church "covered dish suppers" in which blacks and whites ate at the same table.[39] Meanwhile, a number of Baptist women's groups were continuing to support Jordan's approach to ministry. For example, the Kentucky Baptist Women's Missionary Union voted to send the mission $175.00 in 1939, including a very kind and encouraging letter with the gift.[40]

The tension between Jordan and the white pastors became acute when he requested a change in his church membership. After visiting a number of black churches, Jordan began regularly to attend Virginia Avenue Church, a black church that had welcomed him. He felt like a member there and was active in every area of church life, so he requested that his membership be moved from his white church to Virginia Avenue. His pastor was outraged, even citing Jesus' respect for racial boundaries as part of his argument to Jordan.

Jordan was outraged equally, but he was convinced by a committee member to delay his decision. He satirized the disapprobation in his journal, writing, "I guess it is also a Christian principle to tear out of the New Testament all those pages which proclaim the universality of the Christian brotherhood and which so terribly upset our complacent social traditions."[41]

In the midst of the crisis, a special committee of the Long Run Association changed the situation by promoting Jordan to full-time superintendent of missions for the association. He had just finished his Ph.D. and had not developed concrete plans to move back to the rural South. The new position meant that he would now oversee the mission projects and the Fellowship Center, and that he would attend the Broadway Baptist Church, the main sponsoring church, where he was given an office. Jordan was pleased with his new responsibilities. However, he wished the offices were in the inner city because the students would learn to be better preachers if they had "to wade through the shipwrecks of humanity to get there."[42]

As superintendent of the Louisville missions, Jordan proposed a service called "The Lord's Storehouse." It was to be an inner-city store where new and used clothes, household items, food, and Bibles would be sold with customers paying what they could afford. Wealthier churches in the area would contribute, and profits would be put back into the operation of the store. The idea received a generally favorable response, but opposition arose to the idea of selling the items rather than giving them away. Some objected to the plan on the grounds that the churches would be in the mercantile business. Others thought people would not contribute to the store, knowing that the items would be sold rather than given away. The plan was eventually tabled, but Jordan continued to be gripped by the economic implications of his faith.[43] On a smaller scale, he set up a food pantry, which gave food to the needy.[44]

By the time Jordan had finished his tenure as superintendent of the Long Run Association, the Baptist Fellowship Center had become the heart of many community activities. The Center provided a toy library and playroom for small children, boys' and girls' clubs, missionary films for the young people, and a mothers' club for neighborhood women.[45]

Jordan had achieved one of his main goals: to provide opportunities for white and black Christians to come together for joint worship and encouragement. He emphasized the importance of the white church taking a position of listening and learning rather than always helping and giving. He encouraged all the participants to focus on their similarities and common characteristics. Once, in organizing a church music program, he advertised it as an opportunity for white people to see that "the Negro has a great contribution to make to the religious life of the world and that he has an interpretation of Christ that the rest of the world needs."[46]

Koinonia

Jordan was trying to flesh out many of the ideas he saw in the New Testament, including ideas about economics and community. He was particularly interested in what he considered to be the beginning of the church in the New Testament book of Acts. Reading these words in Acts chapters two and four, he longed to create a community that would reflect the early Christian model:

> And all that believed were together, and had all things *common*; and sold their possessions and goods, and parted them to all men, as every man had need.
> And the multitude of them that believed were of one heart and of one soul: neither said any of them that ought of the things which he possessed was his own; but they had all things *common* [emphases mine].[47]

The word common is a translation of the Greek *koinos*,[48] and Jordan was enamored with the idea of holding all things in common. As Barnette points out, for Jordan koinonia did not refer to church fellowship suppers, but to a much more comprehensive "radical sharing of goods, worship, and witness."[49] Jordan reasoned, "If that closeness of sharing in a common life exhibited the spirit of Jesus alive in those men, why not now?"[50]

Near the end of his time at Southern Seminary, Jordan sought to implement many of those ideas about *koinonia*. One group of students, already meeting occasionally for discussion and Bible study, was provided by Jordan with more leadership and organization. He set up a system of economic sharing with about a dozen other seminary students. Each person or family would contribute as much extra money as they could, and then the money would be distributed among them for food, clothes, and other items as the need arose. Jordan called the group "Koinonia," and he led them in studying radical ideas about pacifism, economics, and race, derived from Jesus' words in the Gospels and from Acts. Through Jordan's contacts with city missions, students were encouraged to attend black churches and to volunteer at the Baptist Fellowship Center.

The group, however, was not stable, mainly because its

members did not live together or attend the same church and, as with many students, they moved away after graduation. Jordan tried to have the group make decisions through consensus, but that proved difficult as one of the more important decisions they made resulted in one of the leading couples withdrawing their money and leaving. The couple was in dispute with the rest of the group over a medical treatment for the wife, who was pregnant. Jordan was learning quite a bit about decision-making and group dynamics, and that led him to be more convinced than ever that, to establish the kind of community he sought, a rural communal setting was needed.[51]

Impact on the Church

While the Southern Baptist leaders in Louisville often opposed Jordan's work in the area of racial equality, a group of admirers arose who found him to be an inspiration. During his seminary years, a number of students had supported him in individual incidents, such as the Simmons students' eating in the dormitory. In his time with the Long Run Association, Jordan had developed a larger following of students and local church members. His strong preaching skills and comprehensive knowledge of Scripture made him an interesting and persuasive speaker. Church groups around Louisville often asked him to speak on the issue of Christianity and race relations.

Jordan traveled around the South, speaking to churches, youth groups, and college groups. While some of the leaders in the Southern Baptist church objected to his teaching, many wholeheartedly supported him. For example, William Hall Preston, associate for the Southern Baptist Convention Sunday School Board, wrote this after hearing him preach:

Surely no one could fail to feel the presence of Christ when Dr. Jordan was around. Later in the evening as I listened to him plead the cause of our Negroes, I felt even stronger. . . . He's so strong and firm in his fight for them. I know that his life will be an inspiration to me the rest of my life.[52]

Having become missions superintendent, Jordan was offered even more speaking engagements. A wide range of Southern Baptist groups asked him to address them, including programs at the Ridgecrest Assembly and students at Furman University. Both of those opportunities led to a number of changes in race relations at the local level. For example, after lectures at Furman, students and local church members started work on the race issue in Greenville, and the Sociological Club began a project for better African-American education.[53]

Jordan wrote a series of articles in *The Baptist Student* on race, peace, and community issues.[54] All of them were focused on the biblical texts, to the extent that even though Jordan's writings were controversial, it was difficult for the Southern Baptist leaders to argue against them.[55] It was the focus on Scripture that was leading him to experiment with communal living, but first he needed the inspiration and encouragement of Martin England.

Martin England

Jordan's desire to live out the radical claims of Jesus in the areas of economics drew him to the ministry of Walt N. Johnson. Johnson was an innovator in the Southern Baptist church in the areas of economics and the stewardship of resources. He published a newsletter, and during the summer of 1941, he published an article written by Martin England, an American Baptist missionary.

England had been working for education for the

underprivileged. He had an undergraduate degree from Furman University and a baccalaureate in divinity from Crozer Theological Seminary in Chester, Pennsylvania.[56] In the mid-1930s, England taught at the Yancey Institute and then Mars Hill College, both in North Carolina. He worked on educational changes based on the ungraded Danish Folk School system.[57] Then Martin England and his wife, Mabel, went to Burma to use their knowledge of education as missionaries and returned on furlough in 1939.

Tense political situations in the Far East forced the Englands to remain in the United States. Martin audited classes in agriculture at the University of Florida in the hope of returning to teach that subject at the mission school.[58] Eventually, though, Martin began looking for a farm cooperative or rural community that might mirror the early church as found in the New Testament. He was also very interested in nonviolent solutions to personal and national problems. During that time, Martin wrote the article for Johnson's newsletter that so gripped Jordan when he read it:

> I have not been able to explain away the Sermon on the Mount or the 13th chapter of First Corinthians, or lots of other passages in the New Testament, about loving your enemies. I must confess that there are situations in which I fall far short of the demands of the Gospel in that respect, but I do not feel that I can justify my failure by denying the validity or applicability of Jesus' commands to any phase of life. . . .
>
> [A]s I read the New Testament it seems to me that He meant for those who believe in Him to begin living that way now, regardless of what the unbelievers do. If we are planning to be Christians only when the whole world of unbelievers agree to come in with us, then it will never come to pass.

Here is what I am really trying to say: If the barriers that divide man and cause wars, race conflict, economic competition, class struggles, labor disputes are ever to be broken down, they must be broken down in small groups of people living side by side, who plan consciously and deliberately to find a way wherein they can all contribute to the Kingdom according to their respective abilities. Suppose there were some Christian employees and employers, whites and Negroes, farmers and merchants, illiterate and schoolteachers, who were willing to enter into fellowship to make a test of the power of the Spirit of God in eliminating the natural and artificial barriers that exist now—and let none deny they do exist!

Suppose each would commit himself fully to the principle that the strong must bear the burden of the weak (mainly by helping, teaching, and inspiring him to bear his own burdens as his strength in this fellowship grows). . . . "to each according to his need, from each according to his ability" in things material as in everything else . . . . that each should trust in the Spirit of God working in the group to take care of his needs in illness or old age and for his dependents . . . accepting the principle of stewardship and renouncing the anti-Christian and contradictory principle of ownership . . . accepting the principle of the obligation of the Christian to produce all he can and to share all above his own needs.[59]

The Englands moved to Wakefield, Kentucky, in the fall of 1941 to investigate an experimental farmers' cooperative that had been started by a Louisville businessman. Martin was frustrated by the racial attitudes he had seen in Florida and then Kentucky, and he had heard Burmese people pointing to the hypocrisy of American divisions over race within the church. The segregation of

American churches was evidence that white Christians did not treat African-American believers as Christian brothers and sisters.[60] England and Jordan met while attending a meeting of the Fellowship of Reconciliation, an international pacifist organization.[61]

The two were immediately attracted, recognizing their shared ideas, and they arranged to get together for more discussions. Looking back, England commented that he admired and respected Jordan because "Clarence never seemed to be troubled by doubt or uncertainty at all. He seemed always to have the clearest sort of conviction."[62] Jordan and England confirmed and stimulated each other's convictions on the importance of agricultural training for the rural poor, of community, and of the commitment to nonviolence. England began to be drawn into Jordan's dream of beginning a communal ministry in the rural South.

During his time in Louisville, Jordan became more focused simultaneously on the biblical texts and on outreach to the poor black community. He had developed into a very diligent student of the Greek New Testament. Fueled by his seminary studies, his interest in community and communal living, as well as his social views, became theologically focused. This is not to say that his professors had taught those applications of Scripture. Instead, Jordan himself, through the study of the Gospels and Acts in Greek, was deriving a radical social ethic. He tried to live it out in bits during his time at seminary, but it came to fruition at Koinonia Farm, the subject of the next chapter.

4

The Birth
of Koinonia Farm

Jordan and England spent long hours discussing their
views on community and communal living, race, agriculture, education, and pacifism. They began to formulate a
plan of how their community might look. One might
think that the three areas of race relations, communal living, and pacifism formed the foundation of their endeav-
or. However, the true foundation of their community was
the biblical text. Their interest was in determining the
biblical view on race, communalism, and pacifism, and
then acting on those findings.

The New Testament, and in particular the Sermon on
the Mount, was their intended foundation; they considered Jesus' words, especially the vision of the kingdom of
God described in that sermon, central to Christian practice. Ideas concerning lifestyle, race, economics, and
power structures were then addressed from that theological base. Eventually, Jordan turned to England and said,
"Well, what are we waiting for?"[1]

The pair began making concrete plans. During the
process they considered a variety of scenarios. England

wrote to one of his friends that they wanted "to go into backward southern community . . . and try to bring to bear, in the spirit of Christ, all the resources within and without the community to minister to the individuals and the groups we can reach."[2] Jordan and England discussed different aspects of agricultural life as they might bear on Christian ministry and outreach to the surrounding areas. Underlying all their dreams was the desire to discover the basics of primitive Christianity and put them into practice in a rural, racially integrated setting. As K'Meyer stated, "Letting their imaginations go, they envisioned a rural community center where white and black could come together to rebuild southern society."[3]

Both England and Jordan had had training in church missions work, England in Burma and Jordan in inner-city Louisville. It was natural that their plans would involve a series of programs that would reach out spiritually to the wider community. Mission, whether to the community or to the world, was a characteristic of Baptist institutions. Jordan wrote in his early statement concerning Koinonia Farm, "we want to be humble, rural missionaries."[4] They planned to use the traditional Baptist programs of vacation Bible school for the younger children, Sunday schools for all ages, and home visitations to provide families with spiritual support. In good Baptist fashion, evangelism was central to those programs. Because of their training and church backgrounds, England and Jordan organized their vision of community along typical Baptist lines.

Meanwhile, as the pair dreamed and planned their community, the United States was drawn into World War II. The summer before, the U.S. government had instituted the first peacetime registration for the draft. England was too old, but Jordan was required to register. To make a public statement of his pacifist beliefs, he tried to register as a conscientious objector. Instead, the local draft board gave him a ministerial deferment, much to his annoyance.[5]

While the community plans developed, Jordan was still working as the superintendent of missions for the Long Run Baptist Association. One mission was the Union Gospel Mission, located in the poor white area of Louisville known as the Haymarket. A board of directors administered the mission, and one member, Arthur Steilberg, was a Baptist layman.[6] Steilberg attracted money and spent it impulsively.[7] Although a loner and an individualist, Steilberg was fascinated by Jordan's ideas on community and was in agreement with his views on pacifism. Concerning Jordan, Steilberg said:

> I was attracted by his utter sincerity and by his idealism. He was an idealist like I had never met. He was never anything short of exuberant. He talked to me about Koinonia, but he didn't know how he would do it. I told him when I made money again, I would put a few dollars into it.[8]

Steilberg was soon afterward awarded a contract to build living quarters for the Army in Terre Haute, Indiana. Interestingly, since he was not directly supporting a combat situation, that job did not conflict with Steilberg's pacifist conscience.[9]

Based on Steilberg's promise of support, Jordan and England began looking for land. They searched for a farm that was typical southern farmland. That meant a farm in an impoverished area, where the land was depleted from poor agricultural management, and with a majority of African-American citizens involved in the sharecropping system.[10]

Such farms were not hard to find. Because of the poor

state of southern agriculture, the South was considered an area of primary economic concern in the United States. A number of farm cooperatives and agricultural reform groups began in the 1930s and 1940s, and Jordan investigated a few of their programs.[11] After their initial inquiries, Jordan and England decided that Alabama was the state to target. They systematically examined every rural county with regard to land quality, racial makeup, income, and church and ministry resources. They talked to farmers, county agents, college professors, and government officials. England remarked:

> We looked at some of the best and some of the poorest land I've ever seen being farmed. One farmer showed us a pile of hoes and plowshares behind his barn that literally had been worn out on the land. There was little topsoil and a lot of rocks. The man said if corn sprouts up, you have to pull the rocks away from the stem with your hand. And then when it gets up any height, you have to put the rocks back to prop it up.[12]

With the thorough investigation behind them, Jordan and England decided to look for land in Chambers and Barbour counties, located near the Georgia border, east of Montgomery, Alabama.[13] They were about to purchase a farm in that locale when Clarence Jordan's brother Frank suggested they look instead in Sumter County, Georgia. Frank Jordan was doing farm appraisal work and had run across some inexpensive land there.[14] Clarence and England found a 440-acre farm in Sumter County about eight miles southwest of Americus, Georgia. It looked ordinary, with slightly eroded soil, a treeless landscape, and an old, dilapidated four-room house. To Jordan and England, it looked right, and they put down a few dollars to hold the land until the property deal was closed.[15]

Florence Jordan had been staying in Kentucky during that time because she was pregnant with their second child. Although she could not travel around Alabama and Georgia investigating the farmland, she was whole-heartedly behind Clarence's vision for Koinonia Farm. She remembers:

> Clarence had told me that he would never make money and never pastor a church again. And I had faith in him. Clarence was not just idealistic; he was also sound. No matter how little we had, I never worried about how we would live, because I knew Clarence could make what-ever money was necessary. He worried some about not taking different job opportunities, about whether he was being fair to me and Eleanor, but I told him if he did what the Lord wanted, I knew we would be all right.[16]

Mabel England was supportive of her husband's deci-sions also. She had happily moved to Burma and given birth to three children there, so this new direction agreed with her sense of risk taking. She was not only tolerant, but was eager to see what Koinonia Farm would become: "It was a real adventure to me."[17]

While they were hunting for their farm, Clarence and Martin put together a pamphlet describing their vision. They hoped to raise some support for the rural mission. Within Southern Baptist circles, that was a common way of funding mission work, and they hoped to receive sup-port from churches, Sunday school classes, ladies' aid societies, and individuals. Because they needed to raise money for the entire down payment, they enlisted the help of Marjorie Moore, who was the managing editor of the Southern Baptist Convention foreign missions maga-zine and who wrote for *The Baptist Student*. Moore helped them design and print a brochure and send it to about

500 interested friends, family, and church groups.[18]

The brochure gives a window into Jordan and England's early ideas about Koinonia Farm. It was a work in progress, with little emphasis at that stage on community or communal living. The description of the farm made it sound very similar to Jordan's work with the Long Run Association, but in a rural setting. It was described as a nonprofit Christian mission work which:

> seeks to combine religious training with actual experience in community service. Devoted to the proclamation of Jesus Christ and the application of his teachings, Koinonia Farm hopes to make a contribution to the lives of all those who suffer and are oppressed; who are bound by ignorance and sin; and who are desperately searching for a way in the wilderness.[19]

Their overarching goal was to "relate, through a ministry to both the individuals and community, the entire life of the people to Jesus Christ and his teachings."[20] The specific steps they would take to achieve that goal were:

> To undertake to train Negro preachers in religion and agriculture.
> To provide an opportunity for Christian students to serve a period of apprenticeship in developing community life on the teachings and principles of Jesus.
> To seek to conserve the soil, which we believe to be God's holy earth.[21]

The pamphlet attracted a number of interested donors, but most gave small amounts. Jordan went back to Steilberg when it came time to make a down payment. When Jordan opened the envelope that Steilberg gave him, there was enough for the entire down payment.

Steilberg's business was doing well and, in his generosity, he promised another large contribution before the end of the year.[22] Jordan made the down payment just in time to close on the property.

Throughout, Jordan and England preserved the name *Koinonia Farm*. Jordan was enamored of the practice of community and fellowship he saw in the New Testament, and he thought the Greek word *koinonia* best encapsulated his ideas. As England wrote to a friend, "We call it 'Koinonia Farm' because we want to discover the community of spirit and life of the early Christians."[23] It is surprising to note that neither Jordan nor England seemed to have drawn ideas or inspiration from the many communal groups that have become well known in the history of the United States. Many of those groups had theology and goals similar to Koinonia Farm, but it was only much later, in the late 1950s, that Jordan began to interact with other Christian communal groups.

Sumter County was an ideal location from Jordan and England's standpoint. Outside the town of Americus, the ratio of black to white was over two to one. Most of the African-Americans had lived their entire lives as sharecroppers. The land had been ravaged by poor agricultural techniques, but it was still useful land. It was the ideal situation for experimenting with crop rotation and fertilizers and for expanding the crops beyond the standard cotton, corn, and peanuts.[24]

Sumter County was also an ideal locale for a rural mission conceived to reach out to people spiritually and educationally. Most of those who attended church were Baptist or African Methodist Episcopal, and their churches were small country buildings on back roads. The pastors of most of the black churches were theologically untrained and often poorly educated. The Seay Industrial School and two small schools run by local churches were the only educational sources for African-Americans in Sumter County.[25] For a rural mission with an interest in improving farming, training pastors, and furthering education, it was fertile ground.

Making the Move

In November 1942, Jordan and England were ready to make the move to the farm. The farmhouse was so run down that the men decided to move first to prepare the living space before their wives and children joined them. Clarence Jordan loaded a truck with his family's belongings and furniture and began the long drive from Louisville to Sumter County.

Sometime during the first night on the road, he ran out of gas. He decided to hitchhike to the nearest gas station, and two friendly men picked him up. Clarence soon realized by their poor driving that their friendly manner was due to the fact that they were drunk. After getting a bucket of gas, he expected to walk back to his truck; however, the men insisted on driving him back. Because of the erratic driving, gas from the open bucket spilled on the floorboards at Clarence's feet and fumes filled the car. In his journal, he claims he almost fainted when one of the men lit a cigarette. He arrived back at his truck smelling strongly of gas but—amazingly—unharmed.[26]

Once at Koinonia Farm, Jordan and England attacked the huge task before them. They planned first to fix the house, and then to start preparing the farm for planting. The first task proved quite difficult. The house was still occupied by a brusque white tenant farmer who did not plan to leave until he was ready, no matter who owned the land. Dallas Lee describes the situation:

More bothersome than his skeptical presence was the fact that he acted as though imposed upon and moved with the slow air of authority, as if he owned the place and Clarence and Martin were unexpected and unwanted visitors.[27]

Jordan and England, somewhat taken aback by the situation, moved into one of the rooms in the house, and it was not long before the farmer and his family left. The four-room house, divided by a wide central hall, was in horrible condition. The only water was from a pipe from the well that came into the kitchen through a hole in the wall. It was so overrun with insects that Jordan and England nicknamed it the "rabbit hutch." There were so many fleas that Mabel later scattered mothball flakes under the bottom sheet each time she changed the bedding.[28]

The farm also had an old sheet-metal barn, a sagging tool shed, and miles of broken-down fences.[29] In spite of the conditions, the two men retained their enthusiasm and launched into building their dream. Because of the wartime shortages, they had trouble getting building materials and were denied a permit to build a new house. They repaired the farmhouse as far as possible with the limited lumber they could obtain, and Mabel and the three England children moved in before the Christmas of 1942.

That winter was a difficult one for the England family. Not only was the house in poor shape, but its inhabitants suffered a variety of illnesses. All three England children had measles, mumps, and chicken pox. Mabel was exhausted from caring for her sick family, and eventually she came down with a serious case of the mumps. Martin strove to care for them while Mabel recovered. The Englands' daughter Beverly remembers:

Dad, busy with farming and childcare and never a good cook, began mixing together all the leftovers and calling it "Muckaloochee Special." Being both trusting and hungry, we always ate it.[30]

Although the England adults struggled to cope during the first winter, the children took it in stride and look back on that time with fond memories.[31]

Florence, Eleanor, and the new baby, James Frederick, moved to the Jordan family home in Talbotton, Georgia, about fifty miles from Koinonia Farm. They planned to stay there until another home could be built on the farm. In January, Clarence was granted a permit to build a farm utility building. He used the opportunity to design a two-story frame building with an open-ended shop downstairs and a four-room apartment upstairs; that became the main living quarters for both families. Eventually, the original farmhouse was turned into a henhouse.[32]

Financially, Koinonia Farm was on solid ground. Arthur Steilberg continued to support the endeavor until he had contributed more than half of the $11,000 purchase price. Friends and church groups sent in many $25 contributions, which was the cost of one acre. The Englands were used to living by raising support money, after the fashion of many missionaries, and Clarence was familiar with fundraising through his city mission work in Louisville. Koinonia Farm certainly was not becoming rich, but it was well supported until the first crop could be harvested later in the year.[33]

Communal Living

The Jordans and the Englands were eager to settle in at Koinonia Farm so that they could begin living in a way that reflected their understanding of community.

Florence and the Jordan children moved to the farm in April, and everyone began to address issues of communal living.

At first the two families did not agree on the method of sharing. Martin suggested they live together but have an allowance system and keep each family's finances separate. He thought they could estimate the expenses to be borne by each family, and then divide the income between the two.

Clarence had a different idea of community and of sharing. Having read the Acts of the Apostles, he wanted to base Koinonia Farm on the principle of holding all things in common.[34] Clarence called it the practice of "total community," and it included communal rather than individual financial decisions.[35] The Englands agreed to the plan, and the two families lived as one large family. The two families together made financial decisions, including those to purchase clothing, groceries, and farm equipment.[36]

Clarence Jordan was starting an intentional community based on the complete sharing of property and income, but he had never studied communal groups. Although he had access to an abundance of information on intentional communities, from the early monastic movements to the Catholic Worker Movement, from the Shakers to the Hutterites, Jordan does not appear to have studied the dynamics of communal living. He was not interested in "intentional communities for their own sake."[37]

Much later Jordan gained encouragement and assistance from other Christian communal groups, but in the beginning he used the New Testament accounts of community and communal living to design Koinonia Farm. Joel Snider explains that Jordan believed "the kingdom of God was best expressed by followers of Christ who voluntarily banded together to live out his will."[38]

Taking his cue from the practice of the early church, Jordan placed the sharing of material goods and money as a high priority. Other specifics of communal living were worked out as the occasion arose. One of the first issues to arise in the community was how it would be managed—and who would provide the leadership. From the beginning, Jordan had wanted the community to be governed as a democracy. Decisions affecting the community were to be determined by vote, and plans would not go ahead unless the vote was unanimous. Jordan intended to rotate the leadership among the adults. That plan did not always run smoothly, as will be shown in subsequent chapters. Although he was often uncomfortable with his influential role, Jordan's charismatic personality, natural leadership skills, and vision for the community rendered him the unofficial leader.[39]

Jordan could have used his position to guide Koinonia Farm with a heavy hand, but he resisted. One suggestion of that lies in his emphasis on maintaining some room for individuality within the community. As soon as homes were made available, each family had private family space. They did not live in barracks or large communal buildings, as many other communal groups did. Breakfast and supper were taken in homes, while dinner at noon was the only communal meal. Such privacy and individuality became more important as greater numbers of people began participating in life at Koinonia Farm.

❋ ❋ ❋

The way Jordan and England went about creating Koinonia Farm reinforces the idea that their main motivation was theological. As both their written materials about Koinonia Farm and their actions show, both men were pointing to Jesus. They were trying to flesh out New

Testament Christianity in the twentieth century.

Perhaps what they did *not* do shows that just as much as what they *did* do. They did not seek out other communal groups or research the history of communalism in the United States; they did not look to other interracial endeavors for inspiration; they did not pursue any of the many pacifist farming groups, such as the Mennonites. Instead, they looked only to the Gospels and Acts for their model. One can certainly argue that they unwittingly incorporated much of their own Baptist and southern culture, and they were not consistent in their application of the Gospels and Acts, but their intention was to imitate the biblical model.

5

The 1940s

Farming

Once the Jordans and the Englands were settled at Koinonia Farm, they began the difficult task of farming. The earth was dry and hard, and the soil in poor condition, but Clarence and Martin launched into farm life with great enthusiasm. Clarence had an undergraduate degree in agriculture, and Martin had done some farm work when he was a child; however, neither man knew much about the practical, hands-on, day-to-day running of a farm. Both were willing to work hard, and they did. That first winter before the women arrived, they repaired many of the fences and planted a variety of trees, including apple, pecan, peach, walnut, pear, plum, fig, apricot, nectarine, chestnut, and persimmon.[1]

At the beginning, they did not own a work animal or tractor, so Clarence and Martin took turns hitching each other to farm equipment meant for mules—one pulled the plow while the other steered.[2] Using that method, they cleared the tough Bermuda grass from part of the yard and started a garden. Despite their unorthodox methods, they raised turnips, cabbage, and spinach in the first year.[3] Nearby farmers laughed at the two preachers, so obviously inexperienced at farming, but it gave the pair an opportunity to meet their neighbors.

Jordan told people that during that year he went up on the roof to see what the local farmers were doing. "If they were plowing, we plowed. If they were planting, we planted."[4] Eventually they learned to read the weather and the seasons, and with Clarence's agricultural knowledge, they became relatively successful farmers. Joel Snider says, "[W]ith a tremendous amount of work, determination, and commitment, the land they had purchased slowly became a farm."[5]

In addition to planting crops, they began raising chickens. Clarence had surveyed the area and found a lack of domestic poultry products in Sumter County. He had made a considerable study of poultry in college and thought Koinonia Farm should concentrate on the egg business as its main source of income. Because there was room for expansion in the area, he also saw the chicken and egg business as an avenue for potential cooperative work with neighboring farmers and sharecroppers.

Once they were granted a building permit, local farmer Rob Hamilton helped Clarence and Martin build a chicken house. England remembers: "We figured we could live in tumble-down houses, but if those hens were going to produce, they had to have good housing." Mabel England remarked, "I begged them several times to put me in the new chicken house. It didn't leak, it was well heated, and it would seat two thousand!"[6] As they were getting started, a Mennonite poultry farmer in Virginia sent five hundred chicks, and a friend donated another fifty.

The Koinonia Farm poultry business was very successful. When those donated chicks grew into hens, they produced more eggs than the average in the area, and the high production got the attention of local farmers. One neighbor came by to look at the chicken house and walked slowly around, looking into every opening and stooping down low. When Jordan asked what he was looking for, the farmer replied:

> They told me you had some kind of a special nest with a chute under it that rolled the egg right out to a basket, and when the hen stands up and looks to see her egg, she thinks she hasn't laid one so she sits down and lays another.[7]

Clarence and Martin were not tricking their hens; they were just using good feed and keeping the hens warm and dry.

Nonviolence

Jordan's nonviolent approach, and particularly his advocacy of pacifism, was a hot topic in Americus, Georgia, as World War II continued. The war was an opportunity for southern men to show that they were tough, honorable, and willing to fight for their country. The rest of the United States often viewed the South as full of lazy illiterates, but World War II placed the South in a position to demonstrate its patriotism and courage.

In July 1942, *Life* ran an article making the point that southern soldiers were fearless fighters and the backbone of the military. The *Life* article, titled "The Fighting South: It Knows that War Is Hell but that Hell Is Better Than Dishonor,"[8] made the South particularly proud of its soldiers. Southern youth were so eager to enlist that one Alabama congressman claimed that "they had to start selective service to keep our southern boys from filling up the Army."[9]

Jordan's pacifist stand went against, not only the general views of the people in the rural South, but also against the great patriotism that was sweeping the South and giving its soldiers a place of honor. That patriotism hearkened back to the fierce southern pride at the time of the Civil War. Near the beginning of his ministry, Jordan spoke on brotherhood and pacifism in a southern church. An elderly woman marched up to him afterward and declared, "I want you to know that my grandfather fought in the Civil War, and I'll never believe a word you say." Jordan responded, "Ma'am, your choice seems quite clear. It is whether you will follow your granddaddy or Jesus Christ."[10]

Southern pride did not deter Clarence. He had tried to register as a conscientious objector, but the draft board registered him as exempt due to the fact that he was a minister.[11] Although a pacifist, he did not believe he was passively accepting his circumstances. Jordan explained his nonviolent approach to fighting racism in this story from his life:

An old farmer stated to him with obvious distaste: "I heard you won't fight."

Clarence replied: "Who told you that? We sure will fight."

Surprised, the farmer said: "Well, you won't go in the Army, will you?"

Clarence said: "No, we don't fight that way. Let me explain. You see that mule over there? Well, if that mule bit you, you wouldn't bite it back, would you?"

"Nope," the farmer allowed, "I'd hit him with a two-by-four."

"Exactly," Clarence replied. "You wouldn't let that mule set the level of your encounter with him. You would get a weapon a mule couldn't use and knock his brains out. That's what Christians are supposed to do— they are supposed to use weapons of love and peace and goodwill, weapons that the enemy can't handle."[12]

Simply because he was committed to nonviolence did not mean Jordan was never angry. More than once Jordan asked people if they would like him to put his "Christianity on hold for 15 minutes and beat the tar" out of some racist person. Most of the time he did not mean it. He was using the suggestion for shock value.

Racial Tension Begins

Soon after Jordan and England began farming, they hired a local black farmer to help them. The man had been a sharecropper, and he was being forced to remain in Sumter County until he paid his debts to his former employer. As part of their normal, daily activities, Jordan and England provided a noon meal for their worker and ate with him. Neighbors began to realize that the residents of Koinonia Farm were breaking the local traditions of racial separation.[13] England, looking back on the practice, said:

> We knew there would be hostility. I think what we hoped was that we could make a witness from the beginning and yet not completely alienate ourselves from our neighbors—that we could get to know each other as people. We knew there were some things we hoped eventually to do that we just couldn't do in the beginning. But we also knew there were some compromises we couldn't make. We knew, for example, that we couldn't set the precedent of eating apart from our black friend and then hope to do otherwise later.[14]

People in the neighborhood heard that the Jordans and Martins shared meals with a black man, and it resulted in the first of many confrontations on the issue of race. Dallas Lee describes the incident:

Word got around quickly that those preachers were sharing their table with a black man. And one evening as Clarence was standing in the yard, a delegation arrived at the farm with the obvious intent of acting so utterly menacing that the two men would repent on the spot.

As they stepped from their car, one of the men looked at Clarence and said: "We're looking for Clarence Jordan." Clarence identified himself as the others gathered around him silently. He smiled and nodded toward each of them expectantly. No small talk broke the icy silence, however. The spokesman for the group looked Clarence square in the eye and said: "We understand you been taking your meals with the nigger."

Taken aback momentarily, Clarence replied softly. "Well, now, at lunchtime we usually eat with a man we've hired."

Having so deftly wrung a confession from Clarence, the spokesman for the group jumped right to the point and blustered out what they had come to say. "We're from the Ku Klux Klan," he stated, "and we're here to tell you we don't allow the sun to set on anybody who eats with niggers."

There was a tense pause while this soaked in, and Clarence took just a moment to glance at the horizon and note that the sun was ever-so-perceptibly moving on down to its setting position right then. Looking back into the leather-skinned face of antagonist, which was still cocked with jutting jaw in the concluding gesture of his threat, Clarence cleared his throat and extended the pause to search for a meaningful response.

He knew these kinds of people. He was a southerner, and he was struggling now to make his living the same way they did. In a stroke of inspiration he reached out and seized the man's hand and began shaking it, saying with his best big brother grin: "I'm a Baptist preacher and I just graduated from the Southern Baptist Seminary. I've heard about people who had power over the sun, but I never hoped to meet one."

There was another pause, accentuated this time by the two hands pumping up and down in the air. The man gawked at Clarence in a petrified moment of disbelief, and then he said: "I'm a son of a—I'm a son of a Baptist preacher myself."

And so they talked and laughed and the old sun went right on down.[15]

Stories like this may make it appear that all the tension was brief and all the stories had happy, and even funny, endings. Jordan certainly had a good sense of humor about those incidents, but many were annoying, intimidating, and unnerving. He encouraged the residents of Koinonia Farm to face the problems with politeness and nonviolence.

Martin England recalled a situation in which two men drove by him while he was hoeing near the road. One of the men was known to be hostile to Koinonia Farm, and the men stopped their car and called for England to get in the car with them. "I simply refused politely and kept hoeing," he said.[16] The men drove on, but England had begun to feel the fear of violence that stayed with Koinonia Farm for many years. Jordan commented on this fear, saying:

It was not a question of whether or not we were to be scared, but whether or not we would be obedient. The revelation in the New Testament that God is no respecter of persons, that he is a God blind to externalities, was clear. There was no quarrel about it, and yet the church had just set this idea aside. We felt that whatever we did, we had to give this project to God on his terms. We knew this flew in the face of the southern code. We knew white men could disappear just like black men. It scared the hell out of us, but the alternative was to not do it, and that scared us more.[17]

A number of locals began to look for some way to drive the members of Koinonia Farm away. As the Jordan and England children participated in the public schools and as Clarence's work on behalf of black education became known, the county superintendent of education made his opposition known to the larger community. He was not only angered by the pacifist stance of Koinonia Farm, but he felt infuriated and threatened by Jordan's efforts to make sure black children were able to get to school in bad weather. The superintendent had resisted busing for black children, making it clear that he considered it important to the Sumter County economy to keep African-Americans undereducated, thereby providing a cheap workforce.[18]

In response to that , Jordan and England had requested and been granted extra gas ration stamps to take black children to school. The superintendent, along with the board of education, protested to the rationing board, but their protests were disregarded.[19]

As if that were not irritating enough for Jordan, the superintendent wrote a very upsetting letter to Clarence's ailing father. Mr. Jordan was in poor health, having suffered a heart attack in 1940. The letter indicated that Clarence was "endangering his family" through his work at Koinonia, and it encouraged Mr. Jordan to convince Clarence to move back to Talbotton.[20]

Clarence became aware of the letter when he stopped to visit family members while on a speaking tour and was greeted with great concern. Clarence was so angry that he stormed back to Americus and marched into the

superintendent's office, strongly warning the superintendent never to contact his father again. "If you do, I'll have
to ask the Lord Jesus to forgive me for about ten minutes
while I beat the hell out of you," Clarence told the man.[21]
Clarence considered the incident "one of the times I came
nearest to losing my faith," because he saw the potential
for evil in the human heart, including his own.[22]

Accusations of Spying

During the early years, Koinonia Farm members were
looked upon with suspicion because of their unusual
way of life. During World War II, many in the area
thought the members of Koinonia Farm—with their communal living and sharing of property—were spies.[23] The
Englands' son John had a stamp collection that included
stamps from Burma and Japan. When he showed them to
his friends in the third grade, school officials became suspicious. Through school contacts, a rumor spread that the
Englands were about to be investigated for possible anti-
American activities. Members of Koinonia Farm tried to
clear up the misunderstanding, but their protests only
fueled speculation.

One day a military officer arrived at Koinonia Farm in
a government car with a Navy seal on the side. Mabel,
hair in curlers and a little nervous, called Martin in from
the field and then went out to meet the young Navy lieutenant. She welcomed the man into her house and began
chatting about her travels in Burma. The officer was obviously interested in Burma and had come to question the
Englands about their time overseas.

Martin later remarked, "[H]e was getting information
about Upper Burma from a long list of people who had
lived or worked there. The Japanese by that time had
occupied that area, and little was known about it."[24] The
Englands were not being investigated as spies; they were

being asked to help the United States war effort. As a pacifist, Martin hoped that the information he gave the officer would not be used to assist in bombing areas of Burma.

A few months later, he received a letter with no return address that offered him a job with "strategic importance."[25] Again, the Englands were not suspected of being foreign spies; instead, they were being recruited to work for the United States government, possibly as spies. Martin did not pursue the government work to which the letter so mysteriously alluded, as he had "more pressing responsibilities—he was in charge of the vegetable garden."[26]

During World War II, the war effort brought the country together and infected the South with a "patriotic fever."[27] Pacifists were treated with contempt and hatred, as though they were traitors. The opposition to war espoused by members of Koinonia Farm led to suspicion by the locals. Although Koinonia Farm members were not involved in actively protesting the war, the beliefs of Koinonia Farm members slowly came to the notice of the people of Sumter County. In 1944, Florence asked that the Jordans' daughter be excused from a school play that encouraged the sale of war bonds.[28] The Jordans felt that any actions that supported the conflict between nations stood against the teachings of Jesus. The result, however, was a new round of rumors about the members of Koinonia Farm being German spies.[29]

Koinonia Grows

From its beginning, men and women began visiting Koinonia Farm.[30] Clarence Jordan was well known among Baptist college students for his views on racial reconciliation, and he was frequently a speaker at student meetings and retreats. Young white students were interested in finding out more about Koinonia Farm and Jordan's approach to the Christian life. Two Auburn University students, Henry Dunn and Howard Johnson, visited in February 1943. Johnson had heard Jordan speak on his interpretation of the Sermon on the Mount at the Ridgecrest Baptist Assembly.[31] Remembering that new interpretation of racial reconciliation, Johnson said:

> This was such an eye-opener. There was a terrific discussion in the final session, I remember, over whether or not Negro students should be invited to those conferences. I had already begun to question the compatibility of segregation with Christianity, but this was the first minister I had ever seen who stood up in public to take a position like this.[32]

After the conference, Johnson was so intrigued by Jordan's description of Koinonia Farm that he wrote to him. Jordan explained some of his vision for Koinonia Farm to Johnson:

> When we feel that we are a part of the community and are accepted as such, we'll try to bring in some of the principles we cherish. In this way, it will be growth from within, rather than being a system imposed from without. As soon as conditions will permit, we want to bring in others, such as a doctor, nurse, agriculturists, mechanics, etc., so as to make the community self-supporting and dominated and pervaded by the Spirit of the Lord.[33]

Johnson remembers his first visit to the farm, remarking that "we slept on the kitchen floor of that old farmhouse."[34] Soon after his visit, Howard joined the Air Force "without questioning the decision."[35] However, his Koinonia experience remained with him.

Not long after Howard Johnson and Henry Dunn's visit, Jordan spoke at a religious emphasis week at Stetson University in Florida. Student Harry Atkinson heard him and was moved by his words. Atkinson remarked:

> So many of us in those days had studied and been moved by the ideas of the New Testament, but we faced a real struggle in trying to live them out. Clarence came and I was really attracted to his brotherhood and peace themes. Even though I was exempt from the wartime draft, my conscience was not satisfied. After hearing Clarence, I began to define clearer positions for myself.[36]

The following summer, Jordan spoke at the Ridgecrest Baptist Assembly for their annual student week, and Atkinson traveled to hear him again. Atkinson comments, "Friends of missionaries to Africa were visiting, but they were not allowed to stay on the assembly grounds. Clarence raised sand over this, and it really pushed me to his position."[37] Atkinson visited Koinonia Farm that summer and was so moved by his experience there that he knew he would return. In the fall of 1944, he dropped out of school and moved to Koinonia. He left to take classes during the winter quarter of that year, and then returned in March 1945. Although a little skeptical of the idea of communal living, he was very interested in seeing what might happen at the farm. Atkinson contributed his few dollars to the common bank account and became a part of the community.

The following June, he left with tuition money from Koinonia for Southwestern Baptist Theological Seminary in Fort Worth, Texas. He said, "I had come to Koinonia with very little assets, but I had given them. So the community was taking responsibility for me. I worked, but I had the assurance of knowing that I could write for money if I needed to."[38]

As Atkinson was leaving for Fort Worth, Jordan teased him about a former girlfriend, saying, "Don't go out there and marry the first pretty girl you meet."[39] Atkinson was still hurting from a broken relationship with a girl at Stetson, and he admitted he was pretty angry as he drove out of the Koinonia Farm driveway. "That really riled me up," he remembered. "I was sensitive about that. But the funny thing was, the first girl I met in Texas was Allene Griffin, who worked in the registrar's office at the school. I married her three years later."[40]

In the fall of 1944, when Atkinson was first moving to Koinonia Farm, the Englands were returning to the mission field. With the war almost over, the American Baptist Mission Board asked Martin and Mabel to go to Cornell University for training, in anticipation of returning to the mission field.[41] The work in Burma was the Englands' first priority; with great sorrow, they agreed to leave Koinonia Farm. While there were a number of visitors to Koinonia, the Jordans were the only permanent members for a few years.

Willie Pugh was the next person to live at Koinonia Farm and the first single female guest of Koinonia Farm who expressed an interest in staying. Pugh had been the president of the Baptist Student Union at Blue Mountain College in Mississippi, where she had heard Jordan speak. Pugh described herself as a person who had always done what her family, southern culture, and the Baptist church had expected of a woman.[42] She had prepared to be a teacher, but after hearing Jordan, she knew she had to see what Koinonia was all about. Pugh came to live at the farm in 1948, and was a stable member of the community until shortly after she married C. Z. Ballard.[43]

Conrad Browne, described by Dallas Lee as "an articulate, liberal young minister,"[44] had heard Jordan when Browne was working for the National Service Board for Religious Objectors in 1944. Browne went on to the University of Chicago Divinity School, but Jordan's words and ideas remained at the front of his thinking. "I wrote so much about Koinonia in my papers at the University of Chicago," said Browne, "that one of the professors asked me if I couldn't write about something else."[45] Con Browne, with his wife, Ora, wrote to Jordan in 1949: "I have been grappling with communal ideas for six years at least. I feel we must seek a spiritual family like Koinonia."[46] The Brownes moved to Koinonia Farm later that year.[47]

Ministries Begin

The Jordans and Englands began a number of ministries to the community when they arrived in the early 1940s. They held vacation Bible school and Sunday school classes for children in the neighborhood. Most of the children who attended were African-Americans, and it was one of the few ministries that was sanctioned by their neighbors.[48]

Both the Jordans and the Englands joined the local Southern Baptist congregation, the Rehobeth Baptist Church. They became an integral part of the church, volunteering as teachers and song leaders. Clarence Jordan preached frequently, and he was often asked during the early years to speak before church groups and make graduation speeches. Slowly members of Rehobeth Baptist became suspicious of his teaching, though. By the end of the 1940s, the members of Koinonia Farm were ostracized—and eventually excommunicated.[49]

Jordan was becoming more and more popular as a speaker and guest preacher. When the Englands left, the Jordans were particularly grateful for the addition of

Harry Atkinson because Jordan had a full schedule of traveling and speaking planned for that fall. He was a speaker for religious emphasis week at a handful of southern universities: Anderson College, Baylor University, Blue Mountain College, Clemson College, Furman University, Mercer University, Stetson University, and the University of Georgia at Athens.[50] As previously noted, a number of students from those colleges came to Koinonia Farm to visit or to live.

At first, Jordan was well received by many student groups in the South. The students were very open to his interpretation of the Sermon on the Mount, the parables of Jesus, and other sections of the New Testament. However, school officials and city residents were increasingly becoming uncomfortable with his message. When he spoke at Anderson College in South Carolina, the college newspaper carried a negative editorial. Joel Snider cites this incident as "the beginning of the end of Jordan's popularity in Southern Baptist circles."[51]

Invitations to local college groups declined in number. Even when student groups wanted to hear Jordan, college administrators began to deny him the right to speak. For example, in 1943 the Baptist Student Union at Mercer University had collected money to "buy a mule for Clarence Jordan's farm."[52] By 1948, Mercer University administrators had banned him from speaking on campus.[53]

Jordan's speaking engagements continued, but the locations changed. Churches, college groups, and pastors' conferences throughout the North and Midwest welcomed his teaching. Dallas Lee writes that Jordan "was well equipped academically, and he had a down-home warmth and charisma as well as a thundering radicalism and jolting earthiness."[54] By the late 1940s, Jordan was traveling extensively, and his preaching attracted student work teams during the weekends and school holidays. What began as a localized ministry to Sumter County was developing into a ministry with a national reach.

So many people came to witness life at Koinonia Farm that "talking with visitors became one of the farm's major industries."[55] One of the visitors was Marjorie M. Armstrong, who remembers sleeping on a cot in the kitchen. Armstrong designed a brochure for Koinonia Farm, and considered herself to have been greatly influenced by Jordan and the farm's ministry. She contributed to the monetary support of Koinonia through a program of small non-interest loans.[56] Through the financial support of people like Armstrong, Koinonia Farm continued to provide a number of ministries to the surrounding community, including teaching agricultural innovations.

Agricultural Innovations

Life at Koinonia Farm was much like life on any farm: everyone arose at sunrise, ate a hearty breakfast, and was assigned work for the day. Much of the time was spent in the daily chores of taking care of the farm animals, tending the garden, and working in the fields. Farm life was hard and days were long but fulfilling. Guests were usually assigned to a farm task, and they learned as much about farming as they did about "Bible verses or social issues."[57] The favorite assignment was doing whatever Jordan was doing. The guests could then have theological discussions and gain the spiritual knowledge they had come for while helping with farm chores.

While Jordan and England were learning from their neighbors about when and how to plant, they were also using Jordan's study of agriculture to improve on the local farming techniques. Jordan "developed the first mobile peanut harvester ... he attached an elevator, bin, and wheels to a stationary mechanical peanut-picker."[58] The result was a machine that cut the manpower needed to harvest a field from sixteen to three or four. That was particularly crucial during the war years when extra farm labor was scarce. Within a few years, farm implement manufacturers were mass-producing economical mobile peanut harvesters.[59]

Jordan was also well versed in soil conservation and agricultural improvement, and he soon began to try out his knowledge on the land. Koinonia Farm immediately launched a soil conservation effort by cutting terraces into the land to promote better water retention and less topsoil loss.[60] Like many in the surrounding area, they planted cotton. However, they soon realized that cotton was a major source of soil depletion, and they began to plant peanuts, which became their source of income. They also planted garden vegetables and feed grasses for farm animals. Their goal was to find out as much as possible about the applications of modern soil science and to demonstrate their techniques to others. One such technique was to use ground-up peanut vines as fertilizer for the next year's crop.[61]

As the Koinonia Farm poultry business did well, Jordan shared his knowledge of poultry with nearby farmers. He helped some of the farmers establish their own flocks, and he started an egg-grading and marketing cooperative modeled on similar farm cooperatives in the South. A handful of white farmers near Americus participated in the egg cooperative. That initiative provided the local farmers with higher egg production, and it also established friendships and goodwill between members of Koinonia and their neighbors.[62]

Jordan also tried a number of agricultural experiments to aid local farm families. Koinonia started a "cow library, from which large poor families could check out a milch free of charge, return her when she was dry, and check out another one."[63] Koinonia Farm also tried a number of hog-breeding techniques including a system of planned hog birthing that succeeded in increasing production.[64]

While sharing meals with African-Americans caused quite a stir among the locals, sharing farm information was completely socially acceptable. Jordan and others realized that agricultural training was one of the areas in which whites and blacks already came together. Jordan built on that by organizing meetings and lectures for local farmers, and intentionally inviting blacks and whites. Harry Atkinson and Henry Dunn organized a seed cooperative among a group of black farmers. Atkinson mentions that it did not attract opposition because the meetings involved "just farmers, black and white, and no one cared much about farmers getting together."[65]

Koinonia Farm began hosting classes on Monday evenings when Jordan lectured on chicken coops, fertilizers, soil conservation, hybrid seeds, and the use of new machinery. At first, both blacks and whites attended the meeting. After some questions and conversation at the end, there was usually a time of refreshments. The farmers, both white and black, were uncomfortable sharing refreshments, and usually one group left early. Eventually, most of the white men stopped attending and about ten black farmers continued to participate. Although the white farmers no longer supported the Monday night lectures, they did not try to stop Jordan, and the members of Koinonia Farm continued to get to know their black neighbors.[66]

The 1950s

Church Involvement

The first sign that opposition was continuing into the 1950s was the worsening relations between members of Koinonia Farm and the Rehoboth Baptist Church. Clarence and Florence Jordan had been involved with the church since they had moved to Sumter County. In the early years, they were welcomed, participating fully in the life of the church. However, in the late 1940s, the openness of the locals to Koinonia Farm ended. While they were suspected as spies and mistrusted for their pacifist views, it was their stand on racial issues that brought Koinonia residents into conflict with their church.

One of the main fears of Rehoboth members was that Koinonia residents would bring African-Americans into their church. Jordan's sermons and teachings continued to fuel that fear until he was no longer asked to teach, preach, or even lead music at the church. There was some talk that the members of Koinonia Farm should be asked to leave the church. The deacons took the unofficial position that no member of the farm would be given church responsibilities.[1] The Jordans were aware that the issue of racial integration was the most controversial of their social teachings; they often walked the line between the church's anti-integration position and their own desire for racial reconciliation.

The Southern Baptist tradition was strongly oriented toward foreign missions. Often non-white foreign visitors were welcomed into churches where they would not have been welcomed had they been U.S. citizens. People of various nationalities and races were well received if they were considered to be part of the church's missionary outreach. While black foreign visitors were not always welcomed, others from all over the world were invited to attend Sunday morning services.

In August 1950, a student from India named Sharma was visiting Koinonia Farm. Sharma was studying agriculture at Florida State University.[2] He was not a Christian, but he was drawn to the nonviolent approach of Koinonia Farm and was interested in finding out more about the Christian faith. On the first Sunday in August, Sharma went to church with the members of Koinonia Farm. Church members were already nervous that Clarence might bring his radical and liberal social ideas into their church. When they saw Sharma, who had very dark skin, they assumed he was one of the black farm workers that Clarence employed. Church members were outraged that the Jordans would bring a black man to their church. They ignored Sharma and refused to acknowledge him when introductions were made.[3]

Florence, perhaps naively, had expected the Baptist interest in foreign missions to override their prejudice. "The man was dark," she recalled, "but he did not look like an American Negro. Actually, we thought the people would be delighted to meet him. He was not a Christian, but he had become interested and he wanted to go to church."[4]

That incident led to strong action by Rehoboth Baptist. A delegation of men from the church went to the farm to confront Clarence and others on their views. Clarence handed one of men a Bible and asked him to point out where he, Clarence, had gone against God's teaching. The man, enraged, shouted, "Don't give me any of this Bible stuff!"[5] Clarence told the deacon perhaps he should be the one to leave the Baptist church, since he did not seem to be honoring the Bible as God's Word. The delegation soon left, but Clarence realized he needed to work for reconciliation. He and Howard Johnson visited three of the deacons, but it was difficult to repair the damage.

Within the week, Jordan received a letter from Rehoboth pastor Ira Faglier regarding Koinonia membership. Faglier's letter stated that the church deacons had called a special meeting for the next Sunday to hear a recommendation that membership be withdrawn from all the residents of Koinonia Farm. The letter included this reason for the action:

> Because of our differences in opinion on the race issue, devotion to our government, and proper relationship to the church, it seems to be the consensus of opinion that members of the Koinonia Farms cannot be retained in the fellowship of Rehoboth Church. This being true, some action must be taken.[6]

Jordan received the letter two days before the meeting was to take place. Jordan and most of the members of Koinonia were scheduled to be out of town then. He discussed the problem with Pastor Faglier, who agreed to postpone the meeting. The deacons, however, insisted on the original meeting time. Florence Jordan realized on

Saturday night that she would be the only adult member of Koinonia Farm at the meeting the following day.

That Saturday night, one of the men from the church who worked with the youth came to the farm. Most of the adults were gone, but Florence welcomed the man. She remembers:

> He wanted to know how we would feel toward him personally if he did not vote to keep us in the church. I told him that as far as I knew our feelings toward him wouldn't change at all. He said he felt that if he sided with us, he would not be able to work with the young people, and yet he did not want to side against us. I told him not to worry about it, to do whatever he thought was right.[7]

Florence began to realize what it might mean to face the church alone the next day, so she prayed. "I didn't know what in the world I was going to say," she recalled. The next morning, she and her children went to Sunday school and then went to the worship service. They sat near the front in case Florence needed to turn and face the church during the meeting.

The meeting was called immediately after the worship service, and the list of charges against Koinonia Farm members was read. The charges included bringing a member of another race to church, regularly attending black church services, making "remarks that seem unchristian" about the church's beliefs, and publicly disagreeing with "some doctrine and practices of the church."[8]

Florence could see that the charges were, in substance, true. When the charges were read, Florence stood and made a motion that they be accepted. The meeting momentarily ground to a halt. To second the motion, someone needed to agree with Florence, and that created some confusion. "They supported the motion," said Florence, "but they didn't want to vote with me. Some remained seated and refused to vote. Some of them were literally neither up nor down."[9]

Finally the motion was seconded and the congregation voted to disfellowship Koinonia Farm. While it was a difficult situation for Florence, it was also difficult for some of the church members. As Joel Snider remarked, "[M]any of the members began to cry, as if they sensed something unjust or unchristian had just taken place, but the vote stood as recorded."[10]

When Clarence returned, he found himself off the Rehoboth Baptist Church membership list, and it had been his own wife who had made the motion to vote him out.[11] After talking that situation over, he accepted Florence's actions as "a leading of the Spirit."[12] Although they were no longer church members, they decided to return to church the next Sunday as a sign of their desire for reconciliation. Church leaders immediately made it clear that Koinonia members were no longer allowed to attend the services. Clarence said he told the pastor as he was being escorted out, "If we're sinners, we need to hear the word; if we're saints, we need the fellowship—in any case, we ought to be there."[13]

If they were going to be forced to leave, the members of Koinonia wanted to be able to explain their own position to the congregation. On August 27, while the congregation was considering a motion by the elders that anyone connected with Koinonia Farm be requested to stay away from church service, Clarence read a statement explaining Koinonia's position. Part of the statement declared:

> It is our desire . . . that it be clearly understood that our absence would be due, not to any malice or lack of for-

giveness or willingness to attend on our part, but to the will and action of the church itself. We wish to extend to the pastor, the deacons, and the entire membership our sincere sympathy in these hours of suffering. We are grieved that it has become impossible for us to walk together as brethren in the Lord Jesus. Truly both you and we have broken His heart, and we all should penitently seek His forgiveness. It is our fervent prayer that all of us shall heed the command of our Lord Jesus to forgive each other "until seventy times seven"; to pray for one another; and to love those "who despitefully use you." May there be a ready willingness for a reconciliation which would involve no sacrifice of conscience or com-promise of our Lord's truth.[14]

One of the deacons was so moved by the Koinonia state-ment that he visited the farm, confessing to Clarence that he could not sleep because of his troubled conscience and he asked for forgiveness. Jordan assured him he was already forgiven. The deacon said he was going to resign from the church, but Jordan had another suggestion. He suggested that the deacon stay in the church but act as a "divine irritant," which the deacon did.[15]

The members of Koinonia continued to search for a church with which to associate. Con and Ora Browne were particularly insistent that they find a local church, and they began their search by attending the white churches in the Americus area. They attended the Presbyterian church, and then the Disciples of Christ and Methodist churches. At all three, they were treated in a friendly manner until they inquired about membership. The Episcopal church was more welcoming, and they attended there until Koinonia became a target of vio-lence. At that point, members of Koinonia were no longer welcomed in any white church in the area.[16]

Common Definition

During that era of life at Koinonia Farm, members began to realize they needed to focus on developing their views of what fellowship and community were to look like. Concerning that period, Dallas Lee comments:

> They were unified around the idea that the koinonia—the fellowship of believers—was the continuation in history of the incarnation, of the life and death and resurrection of Jesus. Their responsibility was to make the fellowship at Koinonia Farm as nearly the body of Christ as they were able. They were sensitive to their shortcomings but excited by their new life.[17]

Koinonia Farm was about ten years old, and the struggles and difficulties of living in community were becoming evident. Unity, conflict resolution, the process of membership, and the level of commitment to the group were the major issues surfacing.[18] Many of those issues were dealt with in community meetings. The meetings were both helpful and difficult, as conflicts, expectations, and personal hurts were worked out.[19] The members were acting more and more as a family, and they could see that Koinonia was moving into a new stage. At one meeting, Clarence stated:

> Something has been set in motion here that I can't stop—something that is eternal. As vaguely as we see it and as dimly as it appears to us, I'm beginning to see that I'm in this thing called *koinonia* for life. Not at Koinonia Farm for life, but I'm in this thing called *koinonia* for life and I'm ready now, I think, to commit all to it, and I think my biggest problem has been that I've been thinking in terms of committing myself to principles, when it seems to me that I must commit myself to

the people of Koinonia who are making the same struggle as I am. It is a personal commitment. I think I'm just
beginning to realize the meaning of the phrase personal
salvation or personal commitment to Jesus. I don't think
we'll ever love one another or have the spirit of Jesus
until it becomes personal.[20]

Jordan had originally thought of communal living primarily in terms of principles, particularly economic principles. He advocated the complete sharing of goods and
property, as he found in Acts 2 and 4. Over time, the less
tangible but perhaps more important aspects of communal living came to the fore.[21]

A significant and ongoing complaint of many of the
Koinonia members revolved around how Clarence and
Florence related to the rest of the community. The Jordans
were criticized for not giving themselves wholeheartedly
to the community. Clarence found that criticism particularly difficult, since he felt a strong commitment to working for real community.

His frequent traveling to preach and speak contributed
to the feeling by other Koinonia members that Clarence
was emotionally removed and not committed to the community. Many resented his trips and did not see that they
contributed to spreading his ideas. Clarence remembered
becoming aware of the extent of the problem when he
returned from a speaking trip in the northwestern states,
longing for home and for fellowship, and he was
received "with tremendous coldness."[22]

Other Koinonia members also perceived Florence as
distant. Each family had different expectations of how to
handle family life within the community, and the issue of
how to raise the children became divisive. Florence in
particular was criticized for encouraging her children to
treat money in an individualistic way and to use anti-

communal phrases such as "my house."[23] She admittedly enjoyed being alone, and she had "an independent strain about her that made her seem aloof to many of the group struggles."[24] That independent strain did not take away from Florence's ability to participate when needed and to forgive when criticized. Marion Johnson recalls:

> [She] held out against a lot of things over the years, but when it came down to loving and giving herself, Florence did it. She could argue with you until two a.m. but the next day it would have made no difference between you.[25]

The issue of the remoteness of the Jordans repeatedly surfaced during the community meetings. At one point, Clarence finally offered to have his family leave the community if it would help establish unity within Koinonia. Con Browne recalled: "Those were painful meetings. We felt, though, that it would be defeating our purpose if we had to have someone like Clarence Jordan leave the experiment."[26] Clarence and Florence made it clear they did not want to leave, but they felt they needed to make the offer for the sake of the community. "There was nothing Clarence would not have done to put himself down," Howard Johnson commented, "but we felt that if there were real brotherliness, no one should have to leave."[27]

The members struggled through those difficult discussions and emerged more committed than before. The result was the first written statement of commitment, dated April 21, 1951. The members signed the statement, and they required that all new members sign it. It read:

> We desire to make known our total, unconditional commitment to seek, express, and expand the Kingdom of God as revealed in Jesus Christ. Being convinced that

the community of believers who make a like commitment is the continuing body of Jesus on earth, I joyfully
enter into a love union with the Koinonia and gladly
submit myself to it, looking to it to guide me in the
knowledge of God's will and to strengthen me in the
pursuit of it.[28]

Koinonia was still a small enterprise. The eight original
signers were Clarence and Florence Jordan, Howard and
Marion Johnson, Gilbert Butler, Con and Ora Browne,
and Norman Long. In December of 1954, Harry and
Allene Atkinson and Billie Nelson signed the commit-
ment, and the following year, Iola Eustice and Will and
Margaret Wittkamper. In May of 1956, Christian and
Jennette Drescher and Marguerite Reed signed it. The last
signatures, dated December 1959, are those of Ross
Anderson and Dorothy Swisshelm.[29]

After studying the commitment statement, the community also made a new model for membership. Up to
that point, there had been very little formal structure to
the membership process. People became members if they
showed an interest, wanted to join, and were accepted by
the group. The result was that some of the members later
realized they had rushed into joining Koinonia, while
other people, only passing through, became members for
a short time. For the purposes of stability and unity,
members of Koinonia decided that a formal membership
process should be adopted.

The community agreed on a plan that would give
potential members from six months to almost two years
to decide whether or not to enter into full membership.
Dallas Lee describes the process:

A potential new member would spend three months to
a year as a novice, participating in the community life,

but reserving his final commitment and the relinquishing of his possessions. He would spend another three to nine months in provisional membership status, studying the scriptural bases for the commitment he was to make and, in essence, taking one last look before plunging into total commitment. At the time of commitment to full membership, the new member would either dispose of his possessions (give to his family, to the poor, etc.) or turn them into community goods and commit himself to the group, which in turn pledged to care for him and his dependents.[30]

It is interesting to note that the group adopted a process similar to the monastic tradition, although Koinonia had little contact with the Roman Catholic Church.

One of the most difficult aspects of the process for the novice was relinquishing possessions to the community. It was the most tangible way that members put their trust in the community. In many ways, it was like burning one's bridges. At one point, a middle-aged woman drove her old car into the Koinonia driveway and asked to stay for a visit. She spent a few days watching the daily routine and thoughtfully investigating life at Koinonia. She then approached Clarence and expressed an interest in becoming a member.

Jordan was excited about the new plan of incorporating members, and he began by telling her about the process. He concluded by describing the final step, which included surrendering all her possessions. Members were expected to enter the community "flat broke."[31] At that, the woman was visibly taken aback and she cautiously asked more questions about the monetary commitment. Jordan remembered, "I couldn't understand it. As poor as she looked, I was really surprised. Jesus said it would be hard for a rich person to enter the kingdom, but we'd never even had one apply at our place."[32] The woman continued to express her difficulty with the process until finally he asked her how much she owned. The woman admitted she had just under $90,000 in savings.

Jordan was surprised, but he stuck to his original statement: she must give the money away if she wanted to become a member of Koinonia Farm. The woman asked about giving the money to Koinonia, and he replied:

> No. If you put that money in here several things would happen. First of all, we'd quit growing peanuts and start discussing theology. That wouldn't be a healthy condition for us. And in the next place, unless I miss my guess, you are a very lonely person, and you are lonely because you think every friend you ever had is after your money. Well, if you put that money in here, you would think we courted you for your money, that we loved you for your money. And in the next place, if you put that money in here you would get the idea you were God's guardian angel, that you endowed the rest of us, and that all of us ought to be grateful to you for beneficence. Now for your sake and for our sakes, you get rid of that money and come walk this way with us.[33]

The woman replied, "I can't do it," and she left Koinonia Farm.[34]

Violence Begins

The 1950s proved to be the most violent decade for Koinonia Farm. A series of incidents, combined with inaccurate and sensational press coverage, pushed the local residents in the Americus area to become more and more violent toward Koinonia Farm. Almost thirty acts of violence were committed against Koinonia Farm members and property between 1956 and 1959.[35] One of the first incidents emphasizes the problem caused by the press.

In 1956, Jordan was asked to recommend two black students who wanted to enroll in the Georgia State College of Business in Atlanta. The Georgia state colleges and universities were under Supreme Court orders against segregation. Georgia schools, however, tried to keep black students from enrolling by requiring a number of items on their applications, including the signatures of two alumni of the state university system. Jordan, along with Harry Atkinson, went to Atlanta to interview the potential students. However, the executive secretary of the state board of regents ruled him ineligible because he had graduated from a different school in the state university system. In the end, Jordan was not allowed to sign the form.

Many Georgia residents were already hostile toward the Supreme Court's decisions, and that incident gave them a way to vent their violent feelings. Koinonia Farm became an easy target. Threatening phone calls began that evening. All the usual local customers, foreshadowing the larger boycott of all Koinonia products, avoided the egg market. A series of petty vandalism episodes left the Koinonia members constantly repairing fences and cleaning up garbage. One Koinonia vehicle was ruined when sugar was added to the gas tank. The signs advertising the Koinonia roadside market were torn down repeatedly and finally stolen; then the market was riddled with bullets from a heavy-caliber pistol.[36]

Minor incidents continued for about a month, and then in June there was another significant conflict. Koinonia Farm had planned a summer camp for inner-city children. The previous summer's camp had been very successful, and the second season was scheduled to open on

June 18 and run for six weeks. However, in early June, the Sumter County commissioners blocked the opening of Camp Koinonia, using a temporary injunction.

The charges to be addressed at the hearing regarded sanitary conditions at Koinonia Farm. On June 8, Con Browne filed for a health inspection so they could correct any health violations. On June 25, the public health engineer inspected the facilities and found no health violations. He made a number of suggestions for improvement, which were carried out by Koinonia Farm. The improvements included making all the campers fill out health record forms, moving the play areas farther from the paved roads, and installing fire extinguishers.[37]

The hearing was scheduled for July 2, during the middle of the camp season, so Koinonia members decided to move the camp to another location. Myles Horton, the leader of the Highlander Folk School in Monteagle, Tennessee, heard about the problem at Koinonia through his nine-year-old son. Horton contacted Koinonia, and they were able to move their camp to Monteagle.[38]

Because of the positive outcome of the health inspection, the commissioners could not continue to charge Koinonia with health violations, but four white farmers brought a companion suit against Koinonia. That suit included new grounds for closing Camp Koinonia that read:

> The defendants will operate said camp in a manner that will be detrimental to morals and purposes, and that they had advertised the camp as a camping program for children from 8 to 12 and that they will be shown live pigs being born and have suggested that the camp and facilities shall be nonsegregated on the basis of sex.[39]

Koinonia Farm historian K'Meyer writes that they also asserted that Koinonia, "violated laws against operating a business which lodged and fed travelers or guests."[40] The trial, originally set for July, was postponed until September 20. During the court procedure, the solicitor general questioned Jordan in what Dallas Lee calls "a remarkable exchange regarding the morality of birth":[41]

The solicitor general pressed him: "Did you, as a child, ever belong to any group or organization which allowed you to see such a thing?"

Clarence: "Yes, I did."

"What was it?"

Clarence: "The 4–H Club."

"Why would you allow children under your care to witness it?"

Clarence: "We have been unable to guarantee absolute privacy to our 40-odd sows during farrowing season, and because our hogs are rather stupid, we have been unable to teach them to seclude themselves during this act. Furthermore, we have read all the latest developments on hog-raising, but have discovered no other way of getting baby pigs than by the old-fashioned process of birth.[42]

Obviously Clarence had kept his sense of humor throughout the trial. Judge Cleveland Rees ruled the issue moot at the September trial, and Koinonia Farm was able to get back to work.[43]

Meanwhile, the farm continued to be the recipient of various acts of violence. On the evening of July 26, 1956, the roadside market was damaged when about a dozen sticks of dynamite were thrown through the doorway. No one was in the market, but the front, the roof, and the floor were blown up. It cost Koinonia Farm about $3,000 to repair it.[44] The market was bombed a few more times during the next six months, at one point resulting in the destruction of the refrigerated meat case. Often carloads of people drove by and fired into the market. A Georgia Bureau of Investigation officer found 55 bullets from a .22 caliber rifle in the walls.[45] On January 14, 1957, the market was completely destroyed in an explosion; the burned remains were left by the roadside "as a monument to violence."[46]

The members of Koinonia Farm were trying to present their views in unobtrusive ways and had hoped to work slowly but steadily for change. They were shocked and fearful when they realized the anger of the local white farmers. Hoping that communication would bring peace, they used the local newspaper to make their ideas public. Shortly after the bombing, they took out an ad in the *Americus Times-Recorder* expressing their regret that the violence should bring shame on all of Sumter County. The newspaper ran its own article denouncing the bombing and pointing out that the use of force and coercion were "the very things that our Southland is being subjected to by the United States Supreme Court."[47]

At the end of July, the *Americus Times-Recorder* ran a letter by Koinonia Farm in which they publicly declared their beliefs and practices. After explaining their beliefs and describing their farming practices, the letter closed: "Please do us the favor of not believing a rumor until you have checked the facts. We welcome visitors, and we will be glad to answer any questions about our life."[48] The twenty-two adult members signed the letter.

Koinonia made use of the *Americus Times-Recorder* for a third time that summer, running an ad in which they explained the meaning of the word *koinonia* and pointed out that most of the men were Southern Baptist pastors. Still hoping that they would be accepted in Sumter

County, they included this plea: "We pledge ourselves to respect the rights of those who differ with us. We believe the citizens of this county will give us the same consideration."[49]

A few days later, the newspaper ran this ad signed by a local citizen:

> If the advertisement . . . was an attempt to make the good people of Sumter County sway from their way of thinking or bow their heads in shame, then I am sure I speak for the masses when I say the result was not reached. . . . I would welcome Koinonia's moving to a place well above the Mason-Dixon Line. If I knew that I were living in an area where the bulk of the people did not want me, you can be sure I would move away.[50]

Slowly, by word of mouth, the local merchants and suppliers began to refuse to sell to Koinonia members.

Boycotting

By August of 1956, the county citizens were boycotting Koinonia Farm in every way possible. Local farm workers would not help them get in their cotton crop. One of the local mechanics would not fix Koinonia vehicles. They could not obtain items from the local hardware store. Grain, fertilizers, and other farming necessities were denied them. They could not buy gas or oil at the local gas stations. Their insurance was canceled. Their bank accounts were closed. Although their credit rating was good and they had borrowed and repaid more than $200,000 since 1942, they were not able to get the standard loans needed by most farmers.

The local tractor dealer stopped selling to them, telling a reporter that he had had no trouble in his business dealings with Koinonia, but that public sentiment had forced him to break off any contact with the farm. One supplier told Jordan, "Nothing personal, understand. It's strictly business with me. I can't afford to lose my customers." When Jordan asked how many customers had threatened to leave, the man replied, "None, so far. But I'm sure they will."[51]

That attitude continued among the local merchants, even extending to suppliers from other counties. The butane dealer refused to sell to Jordan and another Koinonia member. While they could wait for many other supplies, butane was essential to running the farm. It was used for most of the heat, hot water, and cooking. Jordan recorded the confrontation in a newsletter:

> We said our major concern was not to get gas for ourselves but for the welfare of his own soul. We asked if his action was due to any fault on our part and he said no, and that was what made it so hard. We asked why he had done it and he said he was afraid of the pressure. We asked how many customers he had lost on account of us—he said, "None!" We asked who was putting the pressure on him—he said, "Nobody . . . yet." We said we thought he had given up too easily and was not exhibiting much courage, and did he think he had done right. He said it was wrong, and that he had a splitting headache and was running a fever from it. We asked if he were a follower of Jesus and he said that he belonged to the Methodist Church but was not a very good member. We asked if he thought there was any similarity between his position and that of Judas who sold his Lord for a bit of gain. He said, "Yes, but I feel more like Pilate. I just want to wash my hands and my soul."
>
> We said that tradition has it that Pilate is still trying to wash his hands. "I know," he said, "I know, it's all wrong." He said that he would help us make contact with other sources of supply. We asked if it would be

morally right for him, our longtime friend, to ask a stranger to do for us what he himself wouldn't do. He said that he thought that it would not be right, so we asked him if it would be right for us, in time of need, to go to strangers with whom we had not traded regularly when our friend with whom we had traded had refused to stand by us. He didn't think this would be right either. So we asked if he didn't want to reconsider his decision. He said, "No." We said that we would be praying for him. He said, you are doing what Jesus taught, for he said to pray for your enemies and I guess I am your enemy. Friend or enemy, we said, you are an object of God's love and our love. We shook hands with him and told him good-bye.[52]

That story was repeated again and again. Koinonia members decided to ask as many people as possible if they believed they were doing the right thing by boycotting Koinonia. Jordan encouraged a method of handling the boycott that was peaceful—but not passive.

To continue running the farm, Koinonia members and friends began transporting materials under the cover of night in other nearby counties. The September 1956 newsletter reported that gas and oil were obtained by "airlift," and that the cotton was being ginned "by airlift at Shangri-la."[53] The cryptic descriptions were intended to communicate to supporters that it was not safe to tell the places and names of people who were helping Koinonia.

Because of the boycott, Koinonia Farm was without resources and also without an income. By the fall of 1957, no one in the area would buy Koinonia's vegetables, fruits, or eggs. The local grain elevator refused to process their corn and other grains. It was expensive and dangerous to transport their crops to other counties, and they had no place to market their produce.

Koinonia Farm had been selling about 125 cases of eggs each week, mostly to local merchants. When the boycotting began, the egg industry was the first to be hit hard. With the help of local resident Slater King, Con Browne sold some eggs in the black community in Albany, but the sales were too few.[54] Some of the hens were sold or given away, but four thousand had to be slaughtered at the farm. Dallas Lee pointed out the hard fact that farmers "who had cooperated with Koinonia in the egg-grading and marketing industry turned their backs and would not even buy the hens or the poultry equipment."[55]

Although the boycott almost destroyed Koinonia Farm by undermining its financial base, it led farm members to search for creative ways to generate a cash income. The result was the creation of a very successful mail-order business. The United States Postal Service, as a federal agency, was outside the realm of a local boycott. Koinonia Farm began processing meats and selling them by mail order. Before Christmas of 1956, the farm sent out information about its business to supporters. The first year, it had so many orders it could not fill them all.

The next year, Koinonia members wanted to process pecans, which they believed would be easier to sell by mail than the processed meats. However, they did not have the financial ability to buy the machinery outright, and they could not find a bank that would lend them the money. They raised the money by requesting 25-dollar loans from their supporters. They received the two thousand mini-loans needed to purchase the pecan machinery.[56] The pecan mail-order business did well financially and also provided more jobs for African-Americans at good wages.[57]

Gunfire

Beginning in 1956, Koinonia became the target for gunfire, a problem that was much more frightening than the boycotts. Shots were fired into the houses on a regular basis. On one occasion, seven shots were fired into a room in which people were sleeping. In late November, buckshot damaged the meat freezer in the roadside market.[58] Then, on December 26, Koinonia's new gasoline pump was riddled with bullets.[59]

Although the bullets killed no one, there were close calls. One April evening, just as Eleanor Jordan had gone to bed, four or five bullets were fired into her room. The bullets missed her, passed through the wall, through Clarence's chair, and into the next room where they lodged in a toy chest. Clarence had just risen from his chair to go to bed. On another occasion, buckshot was fired into a children's volleyball game in the yard.[60]

The Ku Klux Klan

While in many parts of the United States the Ku Klux Klan (KKK) was seen as a dangerous hate group and was forced to act in secret, in Sumter County the KKK acted openly, often sanctioned by the local government. For example, Charles Burgamy, the Sumter County solicitor general, spoke out in favor of the KKK and the use of violence. When he lectured at the Dougherty County chapter of the States' Rights Council, he stated:

Maybe that's what we need now is for the right kind of Klan to start up again and use a buggy whip on some of these race mixers. I believe that would stop them. . . . I don't know how they feel about it down here in Dougherty County, but I had rather see my little boy dead than sit beside a Negro in the public schools.[61]

Burgamy also made comments to the effect that he suspected the Koinonia residents of blowing up their own roadside market in an effort to gain sympathy from their neighbors.[62] While that seemed like a wild accusation, opponents later promoted the idea to the point that it was widely believed by Sumter County citizens.

The KKK tried to intimidate the Koinonia members by smaller acts of violence and property damage. They burned crosses on the neighboring farms, obviously with the intent that they would be visible from the Koinonia houses. A cross burned in the Wilsons' yard was especially clear from the farmhouse windows. In late February 1957, the Klan met near Koinonia. After the meeting, between seventy and eighty cars drove by the farm, and one of the leaders stopped at the gate.[63]

Margaret Wittkamper greeted the group and kindly asked what they wanted. "Take us to your leader," they demanded. Margaret tried to explain that there was no one leader, but that all were equal. That led the KKK members to respond in anger and frustration. Eventually, after more Koinonia adults had come out of their homes, the Klan asked to buy out Koinonia, offering a fair price. Koinonia was not looking to sell, and the crowd eventually went home.[64]

The Law

As soon as Koinonia Farm members saw that they were under attack, members tried to get police protection. The community was diligent in reporting acts of violence to the local police, but their complaints were largely ignored. Many of the police blamed Koinonia residents, either by accusing them of inciting the violence by their behavior or by claiming, as Burgamy had, that the violence was done by Koinonia members to elicit pity and financial support.

Sheriff Fred Chappell drove to the scene of the road-side market bombing, but made no attempt to put out the fires or investigate the blast. Chappell was obviously antagonistic toward the farm, and he was clearly using his position to intimidate Koinonia. He refused to let the farm put up lights near the road, and he harassed Jordan for placing a night watch at the end of the driveway and for recording the license plate numbers of shooters. He also turned down Jordan's request for regular police protection. He did not investigate the incidents, but he accused Koinonia of failing to cooperate with his investigations.[65]

Finally, after a series of incidents in which opponents shot at their homes with machine guns, Koinonia members decided to contact the Georgia Bureau of Investigation (GBI) and the Federal Bureau of Investigation (FBI). One friend of Koinonia had identified the machine-gun fire as coming from government-issue guns. Not only was the government not protecting Koinonia from gunfire, but also government employees appeared to be committing the violence.

Jordan realized that if government weapons were being fired at United States citizens in peacetime, federal laws were being violated and the FBI could be called in to investigate. Through the course of the FBI inquiry, it was discovered that the machine-gun fire was coming from National Guard weapons. That finding did not surprise Koinonia members because the gunfire often occurred after the Monday night National Guard meetings. The investigations, however, never led to charges.[66]

Conflicts at School

Perhaps the most difficult persecution for the Koinonia members was the violence and anger directed against their children. All the children from Koinonia Farm were teased and badly treated at school. School administrators turned a blind eye, and the children had to endure years of antagonism and emotional trauma. Eleanor Jordan had graduated from Americus High School in 1955, after only minor incidents. As the tension and persecution surrounding Koinonia Farm increased, so did that experienced at school by Koinonia children.

In 1957, Jim Jordan began high school in nearby Plains, Georgia, and his parents hoped he would be better treated outside the Americus school system. That was not the case. Jim endured physical and verbal abuse and threats daily. From the moment he climbed onto the bus in the morning, he was faced with hostility. He recalled:

> In one class a boy threw a knife into the floor right beside my foot. If I sat at the back of the class, no telling what would happen. If I sat in the front, I got a barrage of paper clips and spitballs every time the teacher turned her back. I felt like I entered the playground at my own risk.[67]

Jordan was clear on the point that the children must not be sacrificed for the community's work at Koinonia Farm. They decided to find a safe place for Jim to complete his education. The idea of sending children away to school followed the model of many Baptist missionaries. A number of friends of Koinonia Farm offered to take Jim in, including the Nelsons and the Johnsons who had moved to Bruderhof communities. Jim chose to live with the Maendel family at the Forest River Hutterite community near Inkster, North Dakota, where he finished high school.[68]

Nationwide Support

In 1956 and 1957, the national press became aware of the problems in Sumter County. *Time*, *Newsweek*, and

Redbook reported the incidents of violence at Koinonia Farm.[69] Then *The Christian Century* ran a number of articles that reported the bombing and boycotting of Koinonia Farm.[70] Nationwide support came from Christian churches and organizations, beginning with a flood of letters. Many people sent financial assistance or asked how they could help. The October Koinonia newsletter, which was sent to all those interested in supporting the farm's work, suggested ways to help and included a request for people to visit Koinonia and consider joining. About two thousand people received the letter, which recruited "carpenters, painters, doctors, dentists, bricklayers, day laborers, and general farm workers." [71]

One way that supporters were encouraged to help was by making loans to the farm. As with most farmers in the area, each year Koinonia borrowed $12,000 to $16,000 from the bank. The money was used for seed, fertilizer, feed, and machinery, usually at about 8 percent interest. The local banks had refused Koinonia its regular loans, so gifts and loans from friends of Koinonia provided for the farm's financial needs.[72]

The Search for Community

Faced with the financial obstacles, violence, and persecution, Koinonia members wrestled with the question of staying. All the members spent ten full days discussing the possibilities. It was pointed out that it would be easy to sell the farm and begin a new community in a more hospitable area of the country.

In the early 1950s, Clarence began corresponding with Hutterite and Society of Brothers (Bruderhof) communities.[73] The Hutterites and the Bruderhof communities were rural Christian communal groups holding many of the same ideals and goals as Koinonia Farm. Both the

Hutterites and the Bruderhof live in "collective agricultural colonies, each of which is called a *Bruderhof*, meaning a dwelling place of the brothers."[74] The Hutterites, an Anabaptist group that traces its beginnings to the Reformation, accepted Eberhard Arnold's colony, called the Society of Brothers or Bruderhof, into Hutterian membership in 1930.[75]

However, in the early 1950s, the Bruderhof members were excommunicated over differences in theology and practice. The Hutterite colony at Forest River, North Dakota, was split over the conflict. Members who sided with the Hutterites moved to the New Rosedale Colony in Manitoba, while those who stayed at Forest River welcomed the Bruderhof members. After more conflict, the Hutterites reclaimed the Forest River Colony, and the Bruderhof members who had moved there, with some of the sympathetic Hutterites, opted to join Bruderhof communities in Farmington, Pennsylvania, and Rifton, New York.[76]

Soon after that conflict, around Christmas, 1954, Jordan visited several colonies.[77] He and other Koinonia members began to consider the possibility of becoming a Bruderhof community. In 1954 and 1955, there was considerable communication between Koinonia Farm and various Hutterite and Bruderhof colonies, particularly with the Forest River Colony.[78]

The Koinonia Christmas letter of 1954 brings out the struggle among members and their desire to associate with a better functioning community:

> Recent months have been marked by intensified efforts to find a deeper unity among ourselves and simultaneously a closer bond with other groups with whom we share our vision of the kingdom.[79]

The letter went on to mention the connections to the Society of Brothers and the Hutterian Brethren. It was noted that Claude Nelson, who had been living at Koinonia Farm and working part-time for the Fellowship of Reconciliation, had moved to the Forest River Colony.

Eventually Koinonia Farm decided against becoming a Bruderhof or Hutterite community. The main reason seemed to be a difference of opinion about leadership styles. Jordan was committed to a democratic style of leadership in which Koinonia members took turns leading and in which no one was more of an elder than another. The structure of the Hutterite and Bruderhof communities was more hierarchical, and elders made various decisions on behalf of the group. Jordan was too much an American and too much a Southern Baptist congregationalist to affirm that sort of leadership.

Koinonia Farm's decision against joining the Hutterites or Bruderhof did not create hard feelings between the groups, and many people from each group visited the others through the years. A key Hutterite who influenced Koinonia Farm life was Joe Maendel. Maendel and his family were members of the Forest River Colony in North Dakota. When Forest River went through its division, the Maendels, and also Alan Baers and his family, remained at the now-independent community in Forest River, trying to hold together a six thousand-acre farm. After depleting all of his known resources, Maendel asked Clarence for a loan of $1,000, which he and Florence raised by contacting friends of Koinonia. After the community at Forest River stabilized, Joe and his family visited Koinonia for a few months.[80]

Hutterites are plain-living people who usually try to retain their inherited Austrian customs and language, and Maendel was no exception. He was often seen about Koinonia Farm in his black trousers with suspenders and a straw hat, telling jokes in his heavy German accent. Jordan and Maendel were great friends; they were also an argument waiting to happen. Maendel had been raised in a Hutterite community that valued authority.

As a respected member of that community, Maendel often gave orders quite bluntly, and he expected his directives to be carried out. Jordan, however, although sometimes intentionally forceful when he wanted to make a point, was generally gentle and unintrusive. He upheld the American and Baptist ideal of democracy, and he also tried to give each person as much independence as possible. Maendel criticized Jordan's leadership style, stating, "As far as I am concerned, Clarence could never manage that farm to make real money. . . . Clarence was no good to manage people—he was too soft-hearted."[81]

Maendel's expertise was in farm machine repair and maintenance. He thought Jordan was being overly cautious when Jordan said tractor parts could not be bought in Americus or Albany. Dallas Lee recounts a significant incident when Maendel ignored Jordan's words and drove to Albany for parts:

> He located the local dealer for the manufacturer of the tractor, walked in, and matter-of-factly ordered the part he wanted. The man behind the counter retrieved the part and began filling out an invoice. The office manager appeared, glanced suspiciously over Joe's appearance, and asked where he was from. "From North Dakota," Joe replied. "What are you doing down here?" "Helping a friend work on some equipment." Then the manager narrowed his eyes and said: "What friend?" Joe recalled: "Well, Clarence said don't tell no lie, so I said: 'My friends at Koinonia Farm.' " The manager stiffened with rage, tore the invoice from the attendant's hand, and shouted at Joe incoherently.

Joe's humility may or may have not been present that day, but his stern German intransigence certainly had been provoked. "I have to use your phone," he stated with authority, and neither of the men stopped him. In fact, the manager stopped raving and listened with his mouth open as Joe pulled a small notebook from his shirt pocket, patiently looked up a number, and then called long distance to Grand Forks, North Dakota.

When he got the dealer for the manufacturer in Grand Forks on the line, he explained his predicament, saying: "I'm down here working for the same interests that I do up there and I need this part. This man won't sell it to me. I want you to call headquarters [of the manufacturers] and tell them to call this man and order him to sell this part to me." He told the Grand Forks dealer that the part could be charged to the Forest River account there, and then he hung up and stood there, his hat jammed down over his eyes, his hands in his baggy pockets, and waited. He knew what he was doing. Forest River had about $300,000 in that brand of equipment.

Time ticked off slowly. The manager and the clerk shuffled papers and mumbled to one another, subdued by this bearded German's unflinching posture and stern countenance. He had to look stranger than strange to them, and they probably wished for the courage to laugh at him or to go over and pop his suspenders, but they just shuffled papers and mumbled.

When twenty-five minutes had passed, the telephone rang. The manager answered, Joe thought with a rather high-strung "Hello!" It was the home office calling. They wanted to know if a "Joe Men-dale" was there. Smelling defeat, confused by such aggression, the manager handed Joe the phone. Joe accepted it with one broad hand gently—he always handled equipment appreciatively—and said, "Hallo." He repeated his side of the story and then it was the manager's turn again. The manager obviously was told to give the man the part—it was already paid for. As the clerk handed it to him, Joe permitted himself one triumphant glance in the manager's direction. Then he shook the dust from his feet and headed for Koinonia Farm.[82]

Although Maendel had been raised in a pacifist Hutterite community, he was not used to the constant barrage of hateful behavior that Jordan and other Koinonia members had to endure. On a number of occasions, Maendel's temper flared and he almost became violent. During one incident, a white policeman spit at him and Jordan as they were walking toward a civil rights meeting in Albany. The policeman was supposed to be guarding the meeting, but he was verbally harassing the crowd. Maendel was furious at the policeman's actions, and nearly jumped on the man, but Jordan quietly pulled him away. "I wanted to give that man some mouthful," Maendel said later, "but Clarence wouldn't let me."[83]

Over the course of a few months, Maendel began to see the situation from Jordan's point of view. The boycott was real, and getting supplies was a complicated, secretive business. At one point, he was asked to go into town to get gasoline. Rather than pulling up to a gas station, he had to follow a series of instructions that kept Koinonia members and the gasoline salesman from being seen together.

Dutifully, he followed his instructions to the letter. He drove a truck carrying two one thousand-gallon tanks into Albany and followed a set of complex instructions that took him to a service station. He passed slowly through the station's ramp, back out onto the street, parked the truck, and left the keys in the ignition. He walked one block to a coffee shop, ordered a cup of coffee and a roll, and sat there, skeptically waiting to see if the facts bore out what he had been told would happen.

Sure enough, in half an hour the truck passed slowly by the coffee shop. He waited a few minutes and then, on pure faith, went into the restroom. The man was there, just as Clarence had said he would be, waiting to be paid. Speechlessly, Joe paid the man, took the keys from him, and walked behind the coffee shop. The truck was there, loaded.[84]

Dorothy Day and Koinonia Farm

Many religious leaders across the United States had become aware of Clarence Jordan and his experiment in primitive Christianity at Koinonia Farm. One of the best known was Dorothy Day, co-founder of the Catholic Worker Movement. At a time when America had yet to see a Roman Catholic president and when Southern Baptists often regarded the pope as the antichrist, it is amazing that Dorothy Day and Clarence Jordan were interested in dialoguing and learning from one another. It is even more amazing to realize that Day risked her life to stand with people she considered brothers and sisters in the fight against racism.

Dorothy Day saw that, even with the boycotting and violence, Koinonia Farm was a successful rural communal mission. She had been trying to extend the Catholic Worker Movement to include a rural branch, and she hoped she would find some encouragement and support from Koinonia Farm. In April of 1957, Day traveled to Koinonia, and during her visit, she took a turn standing watch. In his biography of Day, William Miller writes,

On the night of Holy Saturday, the day before Easter, she sat in a station wagon under an old live oak tree at the gate to the farm. Sometime after the deep quiet of night had settled, she heard a car speeding her way along the highway. Fearful, she huddled down on the car seat—a well-advised defensive action, for as the car passed a shotgun blast was directed at the station wagon. Pellets hit the car but none hit Dorothy.[85]

Miller saw Day as someone wanting to be on the front lines in the fight to help the poor and oppressed. "Dorothy not only volunteered for the duty but insisted on it," Miller commented, referring to Day's turn at the night watch.

Day also spent one day with Florence Jordan trying to buy seed in the Americus area. As the day went on, antagonistic neighbors began to follow Dorothy and Florence from town to town. By the time they reached Albany, there was a large crowd following them. Seed dealers, somewhat frightened, would not sell them any seed that day, and they returned to Koinonia Farm empty handed.[86]

Day's interest in Koinonia existed, not only because of the community's fight against racism and its pacifist stance, but also because of the central place the Gospels, and particularly the Sermon on the Mount, played in the theology of the community. That made Day and Jordan kindred spirits.[87]

❋   ❋   ❋

By the end of the 1950s, the community had dwindled from its largest size of about sixty residents, with about one-fourth being African-American, to three families and a few guests.[88] Most of the original Koinonia members had left, and none of the black families had completed the process of becoming members.

The enduring persecution of the 1950s could have caused Koinonia Farm to shy away from its original commitment to interracial fellowship. However, the actions of Koinonia members in the 1950s show that the original commitment had been to the teachings of the New Testament, not to racial reconciliation in particular. Jordan lived as though loving his neighbor were the most important thing to him. Working for racial reconciliation formed a part of that love, but was not the only goal. Loving the racist became a great challenge, as did maintaining a nonviolent stance.

Jordan built his community on a foundation of New Testament teaching; that is further illustrated by the connections between Koinonia Farm on the one hand and the Hutterites and the Catholic Worker movement on the other. Each group has a strong commitment to living out the kind of Christian faith they see Jesus demonstrating in the Gospels.

One might be tempted to see Jordan as an invincible hero, but his struggles with being emotionally drained are evident in this excerpt from a letter he wrote to a friend from his seminary days:

Deep in the heart of every man is the desire to be loved, and it is never pleasant whenever one is hated. The real hurt . . . is for those people who through blindness, ignorance, and prejudice resist God's love.[89]

Left: Clarence Jordan, 1934.

Right: Mabel and Martin England, 1940.

Above: Christian ministers and students in Louisville, Ky., circa 1940. Clarence Jordan is in the back row, third from left and Florence Jordan is second from right in the front row.

Below: Churches of Americus Sign.

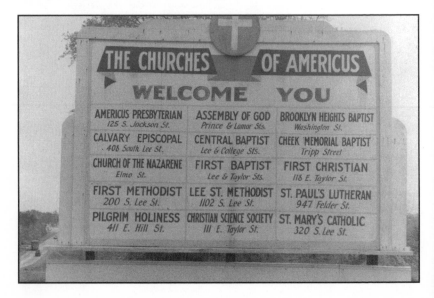

THE CHURCHES OF AMERICUS

WELCOME YOU

AMERICUS PRESBYTERIAN 125 S. Jackson St.	ASSEMBLY OF GOD Prince & Lamar Sts.	BROOKLYN HEIGHTS BAPTIST Washington St.
CALVARY EPISCOPAL 408 South Lee St.	CENTRAL BAPTIST Lee & College Sts.	CHEEK MEMORIAL BAPTIST Tripp Street
CHURCH OF THE NAZARENE Elmo St.	FIRST BAPTIST Lee & Taylor Sts.	FIRST CHRISTIAN 116 E. Taylor St.
FIRST METHODIST 200 S. Lee St.	LEE ST. METHODIST 1102 S. Lee St.	ST. PAUL'S LUTHERAN 947 Felder St.
PILGRIM HOLINESS 411 E. Hill St.	CHRISTIAN SCIENCE SOCIETY 111 E. Taylor St.	ST. MARY'S CATHOLIC 320 S. Lee St.

Above: Baptist Fellowship Center in Louisville, Ky., 1942.

Right: Clarence Jordan, mid-1940s.

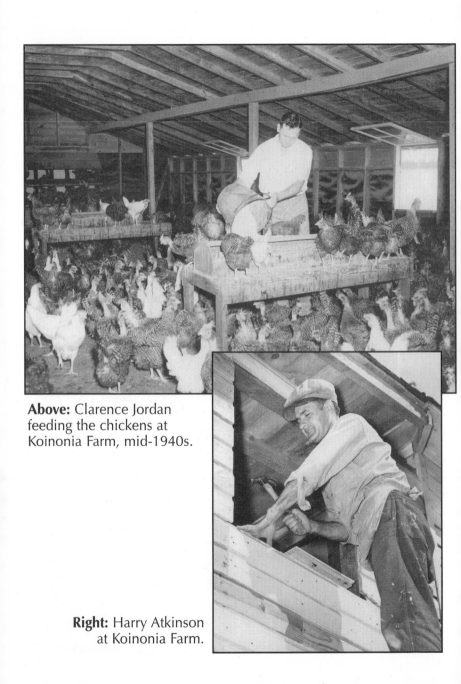

Above: Clarence Jordan feeding the chickens at Koinonia Farm, mid-1940s.

Right: Harry Atkinson at Koinonia Farm.

Above: Clarence Jordan with the chickens early-mid 1940s.

Right: The Jordan family, 1958: from top, (l. to r.) Eleanor and Jim, Florence and Clarence, Lenny and Jan.

Left: Western Pastor's School, Florence and CLarence Jordan, 1959.

april 1970/$1

a voice for the emerging church

Faith/at/Work

THE LEGACY OF
CLARENCE JORDAN
His final interview

*SIGNALS for UNDERGROUND
CHRISTIANS by Bruce Larson*
A HERE AND NOW JESUS

Right: *Faith at Work* cover, Vol. LXXXIII, No. 2, April 1970, Word Publishing.

Above: Clarence Jordan's study shack with superimposed drawing of Jordan.

Below: President and Mrs. Carter with the cast of the Cotton Patch Gospel musical.

Clarence Jordan in peanut field.

Sermons

Thus far, I have been using the history of Koinonia Farm and stories from the life of Clarence Jordan to show that he was intending to create his "demonstration plot for the kingdom of God." This chapter looks at Jordan's teachings found in his early sermons and his first book *Sermon on the Mount.*[1] The experience of listening to Jordan, a fine preacher whose passion for living out the gospel is evident in his voice, brings the listener a new appreciation for the vision he imparted to a younger generation.[2] As a student of the New Testament, Jordan was dedicated to bringing Jesus' words to life. He was particularly interested in making the Sermon on the Mount relevant and alive for the people in his audience, and he often preached on the parables.

The Sermon on the Mount

The Sermon on the Mount had gripped Clarence Jordan since his days in college, and his first published book dealt with that passage of Scripture. He wanted the people to whom he was preaching during his many weekend trips to see the Gospels as alive in the twentieth century. In his book's opening paragraph, Jordan draws his readers in by describing Jesus' disciples in language used to describe America's youth:

> They were young, and life pressed in on their hearts like steam in an unpopped kernel of popcorn just before it explodes. They wanted action, adventure, achievement, happiness. To be sure, they lived nearly two thousand years ago, but that does not alter the fact that they desired to make their lives count significantly.[3]

In the early 1950s, as Jordan wrote those words, the United States was alive with postwar optimism. Although theologians were dealing with the aftermath of the horrors of the Holocaust and politicians feared the Communist threat, most Americans were encouraged by the end of the war, the victory of the Allied Forces, and the stabilizing of the economy. Like the disciples described above, America's youth wanted action, adventure, achievement, and happiness. Jordan wanted to engage them with the kingdom of God as found in the Sermon on the Mount.

His comments to Joe Maendel show the centrality of the Sermon on the Mount for him. Maendel was a devout man, a Hutterite who read his German Bible daily, but Jordan said reading the Scriptures was not enough. Maendel recalled:

> I had been trained to think that Jesus' words were in the Bible from one end to the other, that the whole book from the first page to the last contained God's words on law and order. Clarence just put his arm around me and said, 'Joe, you don't know how to read the Bible.' And then he took me home and showed me.
> He showed me where some of the Bible is just history, where some of it is just telling how so-and-so applied

what Jesus said, and how some of it just sets the stage for what Jesus did or said. He told me there is only one place where Jesus starts giving you orders and that was in Matthew five, six, and seven. He showed me how Jesus didn't talk about community or how to be a Christian—he talked about love, and mercy, and humbleness—and Clarence said if you have these, you have community automatically. Clarence said you can argue about the rest of the Bible if you want to, but there is no argument about Matthew five, six, and seven.[4]

It was not just the ethical principles of the Sermon on the Mount that Jordan wanted to bring into the lives of its readers. It was Jesus. Jordan believed that the "kingdom of God on earth is Jesus' specific proposal to mankind."[5] Jordan held that the Sermon on the Mount was a summary of Jesus' teaching about entering God's kingdom and being a good citizen of that kingdom.

In good Baptist fashion, Jordan began his discussion of the Sermon on the Mount with a call to conversion. "One of the purposes of the Sermon," he stated, "was to present the good news of the kingdom so clearly and so convincingly that the people would repent and make *the great decision*."[6] He explained that the Beatitudes are the stepping stones to making that great decision, which could also be described as being "born anew."[7] He explicitly stated, "Whether we call the process Beatitudes or birth, the result is the same: sons of God."[8]

That demonstrates that Jordan was not primarily trying to convince his readers to live communally, fight racism, or become pacifists. He was primarily trying to encourage his readers toward a fairly traditional Baptist conversion. He was trying also to connect with those readers who had already experienced religion in that way. He considered theology and religious experience to be foundational, and then he worked to convince his converted readers that Jesus is calling them to live out their conversion. For Jordan, fighting racism, living communally, and affirming pacifism were the outcome of being brought into the kingdom.

In his book on the Sermon on the Mount, Jordan made his design for Koinonia Farm evident, not by explicitly outlining his plans, but by explaining his understanding of the kingdom of God. First, he expected people who wanted to become Koinonia members to be also members of God's kingdom; for Jordan that meant people who had experienced a conversion. Second, he pointed out that being a member of God's kingdom would bring persecution. "It's difficult to be indifferent to a wide-awake Christian,"[9] he said.

Third, he noted that people in God's kingdom, not only understood God's laws, but also went beyond those laws to the motives behind them. He pointed out that Christianity is not rules; it is a matter of the heart. Fourth, kingdom members must love, not only their friends and family, but also their enemies. Jordan called it "the road from retaliation to reconciliation."[10] Fifth, people in God's kingdom must seek to be authentic and honest and to fight hypocrisy.

Sixth, kingdom members are not allowed dual citizenship, with one foot in God's kingdom and the other in the kingdom ruled by money and possessions. As Jordan interpreted Matthew 6:24, Jesus "doesn't say that you shouldn't serve two masters [God and Mammon, or money], but that you can't. This is not advice—it is law, as inexorable as the law of gravity."[11] Last, kingdom members must act as though they belong in the kingdom. Building their house on a rock means they have to get out there and build, not just stand around talking about it. Jordan finished his first book with these dramatic words:

"Shall we arise and forsake all and follow him? Our answer shall determine our future and that of the world."[12]

Utopia?

Was Jordan describing a utopia? Certainly leaders of similar religious communal groups have pursued utopian ideals, and that last statement sounds like a call to a new and better world. Jordan could have followed the utopian examples of the Shakers or the Harmonists, or perhaps, closer to home, the Hutterites or the Society of Brothers.[13] His emphasis on the kingdom of God on earth could be interpreted in utopian terms. Beginning an interracial community in rural Georgia in the mid-twentieth century certainly suggests some utopian (and possibly naive) ideals.

If by *utopia* one means generally a better society, then, yes, Jordan was striving for a society, not only better, but also more biblical, as he understood the biblical texts. However, if by *utopia* one means a perfect society or a separatist community, his ideas were not utopian.

Jordan was keenly aware of the sinfulness of human nature, and he did not expect Koinonia Farm to be a perfect community. He was probably more optimistic than the situation warranted, but he was not expecting life at the farm to be easy nor was he expecting all the racial tensions and years of hatred to disappear. At the beginning he was hoping for more support from the local Baptist church, but by the time he wrote *Sermon on the Mount,* he was clear that persecution was to be expected. In the face of persecution, the comforting words from Matthew 5:10-12 may even have contributed to his emphasis on the Sermon on the Mount.[14]

Jordan was also not a utopian in the separatist sense of the word. He would not take himself out of secular society for the purpose of building the kingdom of God. Rather, he planned for Koinonia Farm's participation in the rural life of Sumter County and the Americus area. Koinonia Farm members attended local churches until they were forced to leave. They participated in the local economy until they were boycotted. They sent their children to the local schools, certainly a sign that they meant to be part of the community, until persecution became too severe.

As Cris and Oliver Popenoe stated, "They place great value on service to others outside the community."[15] Koinonia Farm, as Jordan envisioned it, was not to be utopian in the sense of seeking isolation. The farm was, by force of circumstance, led to live a more separatist existence than members had originally intended, but that was not by design.

Cult?

Was Koinonia Farm a cult and Clarence Jordan a cult leader? Again, the answer to that question depends on definitions. Jordan was certainly a charismatic leader, and he did start a rural farm commune. His insistence on the communal ownership of property and his radical views on race and pacifism might lead the casual reader to conclude that Koinonia Farm was indeed a cult.

However, if the definition of *cult* involves a dictator-like leader, separation from family and friends, and the adoption of theological views not supported by the historic creeds of Christianity, Koinonia was not a cult. Le Roy Day commented on Jordan's leadership style, pointing out that Jordan "refused to be 'the boss' in any sense of the term."[16] Although he had a strong personality, he set up the governance of Koinonia Farm so that consensus was the method of decision making.[17] Although members moved to rural Georgia and may have been separated from friends and family by distance, they were in no way kept from visiting friends and family, and anyone was welcome to be a guest at Koinonia Farm.

Jordan's theological beliefs were traditional Baptist beliefs. Although his views on race, community, and pacifism did not agree with the general teaching of the Baptist church in the South at that time, on basic theological issues, Jordan was in line with other Protestants in the Baptist tradition.

Jordan's Sermons

Many of Jordan's sermons from the 1950s and early 1960s have been preserved on tape, as well as in written form.[18] Those sermons provide a useful avenue for investigating his theology as it was developing over that period. In general, his earlier sermons (such as the sermon from the book of Daniel described later in this chapter) contain more of the critical scholarship that he learned at seminary, and his later sermons focus less on critical issues and more on stories and action.

Jordan preached most of his sermons to college ministry groups or in churches, both in the North and the South, and therefore he assumed that most of his listeners considered themselves Christians. He enjoyed making statements in his sermons that would shock his audiences, like this eye-opener:

> You know, you don't like to have naked people present themselves for membership in your church, do you? Because if they do, somebody might have to take the clothes off their backs. It isn't that we object to the naked fellow, it's just that we object to unclothing ourselves. We don't want to readjust our way of living.[19]

Jordan enjoyed challenging his audience by using language not normally heard in church. He called himself an "old-fashioned fundamentalist,"[20] but his interpretations did not stay within the very literalistic method of fundamentalism of his time. For example, in the sermon "Incarnational Evangelism," Jordan took the beginning of the Gospel of John and rewrote it to say of Jesus, "And so, the idea became a human and parked his trailer next to ours."[21] That kind of loose paraphrasing did not endear him to other fundamentalists, as can be seen in their responses to the completed Cotton Patch versions.

Clarence and Judas

Jordan was very interested in the people in the Bible, and he tried to imagine what they were like as human beings. Sometimes in trying to see the biblical characters' humanity, he made some startling suggestions. His understanding of Judas Iscariot's personality and life situation evinced one of those. Jordan preached a number of sermons on Judas, claiming that he found some affinity with Judas. He began one of his sermons on Judas:

> This man that I want to talk to you about is a man whom I perhaps feel more love for, more compassion for, than any other man in the whole Bible. Somehow I feel more akin to him than any other man, and if I call him the man whom Jesus loved, it might be that I'm reading a little bit of my own personal feelings in it because I'm so kin to him that I want to feel like the man whom Jesus loved.[22]

Rather than John being the beloved disciple, Jordan asserts that Judas was the one most loved by Jesus. John calls himself the beloved disciple because he wanted to be the favored one, but in fact "Judas got the major share of Jesus' love," and "John was terribly jealous of him."[23] John was so jealous, according to Jordan, that he portrayed Judas as a devil.

Just as his audience was getting uncomfortable with that new picture of Judas, Jordan gave an illuminating description of his thought process:

> In the Smithsonian Institute, you go up into the dinosaur room, and they've got big skeletons of dinosaurs, forty-fifty feet long. Now, they haven't found that many dinosaur bones lying around. They've found one or two, maybe a tibia, and from that they measure and make projections and make this whole big dinosaur out of the projections from one or two bones. Now if the scientist can make a dinosaur out of a tibia, there's nothing wrong with reconstructing Judas out of two or three passages from the Scriptures, with a little bit of imagination to go along with it. I'm going to put a good bit of plaster in here and there, but there'll always be some solid bones from which to project our thought.[24]

He went on to describe Judas as "an orthodox, Bible-toting, Scripture-quotin' man," and "a man of great social passion."[25] Jordan believed that Jesus chose Judas to be one of his disciples because he was "a really consecrated, dedicated young man."[26] Jordan thought Judas very honest and very faithful—but very naive. Caiaphas had tricked Judas into betraying Jesus. Caiaphas was just about as crafty as the serpent, and Judas was much like Adam and Eve in his innocence. Caiaphas was able to trick him because Caiaphas was a professional priest and an authority figure to the almost childlike Judas.

Jordan's understanding of Judas as contrasted with his interpretation of the Sermon on the Mount illustrates his method in dealing with the biblical texts. His central text, the Sermon on the Mount, must be taken fairly literally. As he had told Joe Maendel, Matthew 5-7 was the core of Jesus' teaching, and must be particularly revered and obeyed. Other less central texts, including stories from the Gospels as well as many of the Hebrew narratives described later in this chapter, were not subject to that rigorous literalism. In fact, Jordan often used an admixture of imagination with critical methodology to produce an unusual blend of interpretations.

In addition, he used the term parable interchangeably with account or narrative, and that causes some confusion as to which texts he thought were events and which ones were illustrations. For example, he treated the idea of the virgin birth of Christ as a real event: that "God has decided to become a member of the human race, that he's joined with us . . . to produce . . . a divine-human creature who will have his Father in heaven and his mother on earth."[27] Perhaps that description does not use traditional theological language, but it does show that Jordan believed that Jesus' virgin birth was an actual event. Meanwhile, in the same paragraph, he calls it "the parable of the virgin birth."[28] Apparently, although a New Testament scholar, he did not use the standard definition of the term parable.

Cotton Patch Versions Foreshadowed

Most of Jordan's sermons that are preserved on tape or in written form were prepared before he created his Cotton Patch paraphrases, but the beginnings of the paraphrases are evident in many of the sermons. His early sermons show that he was already thinking of ways to translate biblical ideas and characters into the twentieth century. He enjoyed updating all the disciples by calling them nicknames or shortened names. John is called Jack, Andrew is Andy, and Peter Bar-Jonah is Rock Johnson.[29]

Jordan's sermons also foreshadowed the Cotton Patch versions in the way he brought modern racial tensions into the ancient text. For example, before writing his paraphrases, he had already begun to see the main tension in the Gospels as between blacks and whites, rather than between Jews and Gentiles or Pharisees and sinners. That is made clear in the sermon entitled "The Mind of Christ in the Racial Conflict," in which he declares:

> The word Pharisee is not synonymous with the word hypocrite, contrary to what we may think. You know what the Hebrew word pharisee means? It'll surprise you. It means "a segregationist"; it means "one who separates himself." "Woe to you, segregationist!" And if we translate it as it should be translated, I think a lot of southern Christians might join Buddhism or some other religion.[30]

Jordan made it very clear in the same sermon that he was not primarily a civil rights leader who was religious on the side. His critique of the racial conflict in the United States was that "most Americans are seeking the mind of the president and not the mind of Jesus Christ."[31] Of the people surrounding Jordan who claimed to be Christians he said, "[T]hey look to the decisions of the Supreme Court, not to the dictates of the Sermon on the Mount."[32] It was the lack of knowledge of and honor for the Bible by Christians that pushed him to write his Cotton Patch versions to bring the biblical texts alive.

Before he had written his Cotton Patch versions, Jordan rewrote some of the biblical accounts using satire to make his point. He called it "the goofed-up Bible," and the main issue was not racial conflict but the love of money. He certainly enjoyed using his imagination to tinker with the biblical texts. Here is an example of one of his "goofed-up" translations, turning Matthew 19:16-29 upside down:

> And a certain depositor asked him [Jesus] saying, "Good banker, what shall I do to become really rich?" And Jesus said to him, "Why callest thou me good? None is good save one—that is Mammon himself. Thou knowest the commandments, 'Do not pay fair wages,' 'Do not be honest,' 'Don't have a soft conscience,' 'Don't pay any avoidable taxes,' 'Take all the interest and profit you can get.'" And he said, "All these rules have I kept from my youth up."
>
> Now, when Jesus heard these things, he said unto him, "Yet lackest thou one thing. Sell all thou hast and put it in my bank and thou shall have treasure on earth; and come, let me manage their affairs." And when he heard this, he was exceedingly glad, for he himself was not much of a businessman. And when Jesus saw that he was exceedingly glad, he said, "How easily shall they who have some riches enter into the Kingdom of Mammon. For it is easier than falling off a log for an unscrupulous man to enter into the Kingdom of Mammon."
>
> And they that heard that said, "Who, then, can be poor?" And he said, "The things that are impossible with men are possible with Mammon." Then Peter said, "Lo, we have invested all and followed your advice." And he said unto them, "Verily I say unto you, there is no man that hath invested in slum houses or government bonds or suburban real estate or blue-chip securities or stocks for Mammon's sake who shall not receive manifold more dividends in this present time, and in the years ahead, everlasting status."[33]

Jordan's willingness to tamper with the biblical texts to make his point made his more conservative readers and hearers a little nervous. It was his capacity for using his imagination and his treatment of the texts in a slightly irreverent way that led some of his listeners to encourage him to pursue the Cotton Patch versions.

The Parables

Two of Jesus' parables appear to have been Jordan's favorites. He came back to them again and again in his preaching and lectures. They are known as the parables of the prodigal son and of the good Samaritan. Jordan translated the good Samaritan in a very interesting way in his version of Luke's Gospel; it will be discussed in chapter 9, which covers the Cotton Patch paraphrases.

The prodigal son parable represents one of the instances when Jordan used his imagination to combine two genres of texts. He combined that parable with the story of the man possessed by Legion. In his sermon entitled "The Man from Gadera," Jordan tells of a young man who leaves his father, squanders his inheritance, and is forced to live with the pigs. In that sermon, Jordan explains:

> I think this demon-possessed man from Judea had been brought up in a devout home and had been taught it was wrong to eat hog meat. But now, in this far-off country, he begins to be in want and he's got nothing to eat and he goes out and gets a job, of all things, feeding hogs. You can imagine the tension in that man's heart as he goes about feeding these hogs, which his mama and daddy had taught him were the worst things on the face of the earth—"unclean, unclean!"—and here he was feeding them.[34]

The combination of living in extreme poverty and having to take care of ceremonially unclean animals drove the young man insane. Jordan described the demons both as devils who "begin to enter in a conversation with Jesus,"[35] and as a psychological condition, without ever choosing one over the other or acknowledging that he is interpreting the same texts both literally and in a more progressive, psychological manner.

He explains that after Jesus heals the man and drives the pigs over the cliff, the man wants to follow Jesus.

> Jesus said, "No, son, you know your old daddy, just before I left Judea he was telling me about you. He said: 'You know, I have two fine boys. One of them's still with me; he's helping me on the farm. But one of them, the younger one, I don't know what happened to him. He got it in his head he wanted to leave, and I gave him money and he left, and I haven't had as much as a post-card from him. Jesus, you travel around a good bit; if you should run across him, tell him his old pappy loves him and would like to have him home any time he wants to come.'"[36]

So the man returns to his father and is welcomed as a long-lost son.[37] For Jordan, the connection between the stories is the pigs. That is an example of his mixing genres: he deals with the narrative (the story of the man possessed) and the parable as though they were the same type of literature. Apparently he did that because he held to the idea that all of Jesus' words must be true, literally true, including the parables. For Jordan, the parables were not stories that Jesus made up to illustrate a point. They were real events that Jesus then used to illustrate life in the kingdom. That hermeneutic comes out of a very literal understanding of Scripture in which the entire Bible must actually be historical, including the parables. However, in that same parable, Jordan interprets demon possession as a mental illness (as well as an actual possession), an interpretation that is not literal and appears to come from his more progressive seminary training. Here, in the blending of two stories, we see the patchwork nature of Jordan's approach to Scripture. The issue is further complicated by his loose use of the term parable.

The Hebrew Scriptures

Jordan spent most of his time preaching and writing about the New Testament texts, a focus reflecting the Baptist theology of the time. Baptist churches were seeking to be New Testament churches. The Old Testament was part of a previous dispensation, but the New Testament was the blueprint for the church. Therefore, Jordan was mainly interested in Jesus and the kingdom of God as found in the Gospels. When he interpreted the New Testament texts, he used a variety of hermeneutical approaches. Having studied the New Testament for his Ph.D., he seemed familiar with a wide variety of interpretive models.

When Jordan interpreted the Hebrew Scriptures, however, he usually employed the critical methods he had learned at Southern Seminary. That was reflected in three ways. First, he did not take many of the stories to be literally true. That approach stands in contrast to his interpretation of most of the Gospel texts and certainly his view of the Sermon on the Mount. Second, in conjunction with that, he did believe those stories told religious truth. He espoused the neo-liberal idea that religious truth did not require historical truth. Third, Jordan held fairly progressive ideas about dating some of the Hebrew texts.

His understanding of the book of Daniel is a good

example of those three critical elements. Concerning the historical truth of the text, Jordan states, "We all know that the account of Daniel in the lions' den—the three young men in the fiery furnace—is not scientific fact."[38] He argued that requiring the text to be scientifically factual would restrict the truth God intended. He explained that Daniel "reveals the truth about God and about man to such a vast extent that if you were confined to just scientific fact, you couldn't plumb the depths of either God or man."[39] In case his audience has not understood his point, Jordan becomes even more direct:

It [Daniel] is not a historical narrative. And everyone would know that Shadrach, Meshach, and Abednego, and Daniel are really not actual historical figures. They are people as real as Rhett Butler and Scarlett O'Hara in Gone with the Wind.[40]

Having stated that Daniel is not intended to be historically accurate or scientifically true, Jordan goes on to state that the book does, however, present "religious truth."[41] In another sermon on Daniel, Jordan explains:

The book, then, purports to be a treatise—at least the first six chapters of it—on what happens to a spiritually sensitive person when his government and his God are on a collision course. This might be considered a historical parable in which the writer has concealed a truth; and the truth is that in the time of testing, when God and government are on a collision course, God calls his people to be faithful to him even though it means disobedience to the government.[42]

Jordan described the book of Daniel as both a parable and a treatise against a king from the intertestamental period. We see his use of progressive higher criticism in the dating and occasion of the book of Daniel. He dated Daniel at about 167 B.C. and held the view that Daniel was written "closer to the New Testament than any other of the Old Testament books."[43] He believed the book of Daniel was not written about Nebuchadnezzar but about the Emperor Antiochus Epiphanes, who greatly persecuted the Jews in the second century B.C. Jordan states that Daniel "was written primarily to young people who were being forced against their will to obey government edicts to which they could not conscientiously agree."[44]

Having explained the book of Daniel in much the same way that he had learned at seminary, Jordan then preached the remainder of this sermon from Daniel as though the story *were* about Daniel and Nebuchadnezzar![45] That dualistic handling of the texts appears to be consistent with Jordan's understanding of Daniel being religiously, but not historically or scientifically, true. I suspect he did not know how to integrate his seminary learning with his desire to plainly preach the text, and that therefore he tried to include both.

❋　❋　❋

Jordan's preaching and writing on the Sermon on the Mount, together with his various sermons, show that he was intent on creating a community based on his understanding of the biblical texts. In particular, he used the Sermon on the Mount as his blueprint for living as a citizen of God's kingdom. Although using a mixture of interpretive models, particularly when preaching from the Hebrew Scriptures, he took the Sermon on the Mount very literally. His understanding of loving one's enemy or the outsider, together with the racial tensions around him, led Jordan to interpret many of the texts in the light of racial conflict. It was his theology that informed his reaction to his white and black neighbors, and it was his theology that gave him the strength to resist racism for years, often with little outside encouragement.

Jordan's use of his imagination in interpreting texts helped his hearers and readers see Jesus and other biblical characters as real people who faced the same problems we face and were expected to fight a similar kind of racism existing in biblical times. Although he called himself a fundamentalist, his interpretive models were extremely varied. Many of his sermons revolved around biblical reasons for fighting racism. One result was that pastors, scholars, and lay people across the theological spectrum praised Jordan's preaching.

It is important to note here what Jordan did *not* write. He did not give speeches about civil rights, and he did not write books with ending racism as the primary agendum. Rather, he gave sermons and wrote his first book about the Sermon on the Mount. It is clear that his goal was to lead other Christians to fight racism because of their Christian beliefs.

Although some of his sermons have an evangelistic element, as any good Baptist sermon would, Jordan was not primarily an evangelist in the sense of directing his audience toward a conversion to Christianity. He assumed that most, if not all, of his audience were at least calling themselves Christians, since he was usually asked to speak in churches or Christian college groups. However, he was trying to convert Christians into people who saw Jesus' love for African-Americans. Jordan wanted people who called themselves Christians to see that obedience to Jesus meant fighting racism. James McClendon sees that for Jordan, faith was "always understood as the ground of action."[46] He wanted to inspire action in his hearers.

Jordan preached from very sparse notes, sometimes written on an envelope or other scrap of paper. Because of that we do not have his original sermon manuscripts as he intended to preach them. We have transcripts of what he did preach. No two sermons were alike, even if they were on the same text or subject. In his previously mentioned sermon, "Incarnational Evangelism," the prodigal son is described as the same man who was possessed by the Legion of demons.[47] In "The Father's Pursuing Love," however, he did not make that connection.[48] While the Sermon on the Mount functioned as a center, McClendon may be right when he said, "Jordan's changing theology was never fixed in a single pattern."[49]

8

The 1960s

Koinonia Farm Regroups

By 1960, the Jordans, the Brownes, the Wittkampers, and the Dreschers were the only original Koinonia members who lasted through the violence. A few new people, including Ross Anderson and Dorothy Swisshelm, committed themselves to Koinonia during that time, and a handful of guests and visitors were always around. However, the Koinonia community lacked unity and appeared to be floundering.

In addition, the years of boycotting had taken their toll on Koinonia's financial situation. Some of the buildings had sustained damage because of violence and shootings; the farm stand was repeatedly ruined and rebuilt; the new mail-order business required money for mailings and advertising; and the grand jury case left Koinonia members under the weight of large legal fees. By 1960, Koinonia Farm remained about $30,000 in debt.[1]

Feeling like personal and financial failures, Koinonia members spent almost all their energy in the early 1960s on restoring the farm as a profitable operation. The Jordans' daughter Jan remembers that the farm was in "survival mode."[2] The changes from being mainly a poultry farm to growing peanuts and pecans and from local distribution to mail-order distribution took a large amount of energy.

By 1961, the pecan and peanut business was running well, but the farm was still in debt. Gifts and loans covered some of the debts, and the farm began raising cattle to supplement their earnings. Farm members also tried growing pine trees to increase their income, and they grew Bermuda grass for the cattle.[3] There was little time or energy for reaching out to the community as they had formerly. There were no agricultural education classes, and they did not run as many ministries such as vacation Bible school as they had in the early and mid-1950s. Interracial summer camp was out of the question due to the escalating violence.[4]

The New Agriculture

Agriculture changed in many ways during the twentieth century, and those changes impacted Koinonia Farm. Sharecropping declined and the model of the farm as a business emerged.[5] Koinonia became one of those businesses. Its members grew and harvested their crops of nuts and also processed them in the pecan plant, packaged them, and sent them out through their mail-order business. The pecans and peanuts were sent out raw, roasted, or covered in chocolate. Fruitcakes and the southern favorite called a pecan nut log were also part of the mail order business.

Soon Koinonia Farm was hiring many people to work in their plant seasonally, and about 15 people were hired full-time to handle the mail-order business.[6] One of those workers, Willa Mae Champion, said that Jordan was "the first person ever to thank her for a day's work and the first boss who asked her opinion on things."[7] Koinonia Farm was evolving along with the economy.

Koinonia members had stopped agricultural extension work in the late 1950s and early 1960s because they did not have the resources or energy to devote to those projects. Many local white farmers were boycotting anything to do with Koinonia Farm, and black farmers were afraid of the violence—with good reason—so there was no one left to attend classes in farm techniques.

In addition, farming in general was changing, and Koinonia Farm was affected by those changes. Jordan and other Koinonia residents were not in a position to teach the new way of farming because they were still learning and experimenting themselves. Jordan's original vision included assisting black farmers, but many African-Americans in Sumter County were leaving for work in northern cities.[8]

As Koinonia Farm adopted more of a business model of farming and as people were hired to work in the pecan plant, the emphasis shifted from assisting sharecroppers in working themselves out of that system to bringing in African-American workers at the pecan plant. The plant with its mail-order business became more isolated from the community than the egg business had been. As a result, violence died down. By the end of the 1960s, Koinonia Farm had slowly become a respectable local business.

Schools

In 1960, the Americus, Georgia, school board refused to allow the Koinonia students to attend the local public schools. Although the underlying issue concerned the racial views of Koinonia members, the children who desired to attend the public schools were white children trying to attend white schools. Jan Jordan, Lora Ruth Browne, and Billy Wittkamper were refused admission to the Americus high school. Koinonia members decided to take the Americus school system to court; that was the first time Koinonia had instigated court action. The American Civil Liberties Union (ACLU) fought for the right of the Koinonia children to attend their local schools. Patrick Malin of the ACLU argued before a federal judge that:

> [Koinonia] members' belief in racial desegregation is part of their religious conviction for which they have already suffered greatly in physical attacks on their lives and economic boycotts of their agricultural products. This effort to block the educational opportunity of three young people is a direct reprisal on the Koinonia community for its free exercise of religion and expression of opinion. . . . Such reprisal is wholly unconstitutional and must fail.[9]

On October 25, 1960, the federal judge issued an injunction requiring the Americus schools to admit Koinonia children.[10]

Although the schools were required to admit them, Clarence wanted the children to have a choice. He recalled telling his daughter Jan:

> [W]e won the case in the court, but there isn't a court in all the land that can make these folks love you. Now, they are going to be unkind, and I'm just wondering if you really want to go to school here. If you don't, well, we'll send you somewhere else. We don't want you to feel that you are a victim of circumstances.[11]

Jan responded, "Daddy, I want to go to school here. I think we got some ideas that these folks need to hear."[12]

Jan persevered even though the other students treated her horribly. No one greeted her when she arrived at school; no one smiled and waved; no one treated her like a human being. She was ostracized all four years of high school. Students would not sit with her in the cafeteria; and if she sat at their table, they would move away. If she sat alone, some students would walk around for ten or fifteen minutes, looking for an empty table, rather than sit with her. She once told Clarence, "You know, Daddy, I've learned to eat real slow."[13]

During the spring of her senior year of high school, Jan came to Clarence at the end of her patience:

Dad, I don't know whether I can make it or not. This little boy, Bob Speck, he's just about to drive me crazy. For all the year now, every time I go from my home room down the hall to some other room this little old boy meets me and he starts calling me all kinds of foul names—communist, whore, and all that kind of stuff—just as loud as he can, and then he just laughs as though he had thought up something original. He does that four or five times a day, and he's been doing it every day during the week since school started.[14]

Faced with his daughter's pain, Clarence tried talking to the school principal, but he got nowhere. Frustrated and feeling his daughter's distress, Clarence returned home and said to Jan:

I'm going to come to school this afternoon. As soon as school's out, I want you to come out on the school grounds and meet me. And then I want you to point out to me Bob Speck. I've tried to be a follower of Jesus and he taught me to love my enemies and all like that, but at that time, I'm going to ask Jesus to excuse me for about fifteen minutes while I beat the hell out of Bob Speck.[15]

Jan did not take him seriously, and she laughed at him. "Daddy," she said, "you can't be excused from being a Christian for fifteen minutes."[16] Two weeks later, Clarence asked her how things were with this boy, and she explained that she had solved the problem herself:

> I got to figuring out that I'm a little taller than Bob and I could see him before he could see me. When I'd see him, I'd begin smiling and waving and gushing at him like I was just head over heels in love with him. "Hi, Bob! Hi!" I'd just go all the way down the hall just looking like I was going to eat him up! The other kids got to teasing him about me having a crush on him and, now, the only time I see him is when he peeps around the corner to see if I'm coming. If I am, he goes all the way round the outside. He doesn't bother me any more.[17]

Clarence remarked that he was both amused and humbled by his daughter's creative solution.

Clarence Jordan's Hero

Many people who heard about Jordan through newspapers and magazine articles were beginning to consider him a hero. Perhaps it is helpful to see the sort of person that Jordan himself considered heroic. In the early 1960s, he was invited to preach at a Southern Baptist church in North Carolina. He looked up the suburb of a large city on a map and decided "it was some swank, aristocratic, liberal church that wanted somebody to come to it and pat it on the back for its liberal views toward race."[18] He had had only a few chances to preach in Baptist churches since being disfellowshiped, and he planned to "hold those folks over the brink and singe their eyebrows."[19]

When he arrived, he was completely surprised to find a thriving interracial church. Black and white members sat together in the pews, sang together in the choir, and even ate lunch together on the front lawn after the service. Near the end of the lunch, he asked the pastor to explain how this church came into being. "Were you integrated before the Supreme Court decision?" Jordan asked. "What decision?" the pastor replied. He then began to explain his church's history:

> This little church here was too poor to have a preacher and I just volunteered. They accepted me and I started preaching. Someone read to me in there where God is no respecter of persons, and I preached that. Well, the deacons came around to me after that sermon and said, 'Now, brother pastor, we not only don't let a nigger spend the night in this town, we don't even let him pass through. Now, we don't want that kind of preaching you're giving us.'

"What did you do?" Jordan asked him, and he replied:

> I fired them deacons. I turned them out. I told them anybody that didn't know any more about the gospel of Jesus than that, not only shouldn't be an officer in the church, he shouldn't be a member of it. I preached awfully hard, and I finally preached them down to two, but those two were committed. I made sure that any time after that, anybody who came into my church understood that they were giving their life to Jesus Christ and they were going to have to be serious about it. What you see is the result of that.[20]

Jordan loved that story and retold it many times. That pastor had the same sense of following Jesus at all cost that inspired him. Once, in telling the story, he commented, "I thank God there was still one unruined preacher in the South who had no better sense than to preach the gospel."[21]

Communal Connections

Koinonia members were, of course, quite interested in the theory of Christian communal living, and developed relationships with other Christian communal groups active in the 1950s and 1960s. In addition to extensive contact and friendships with Hutterite/Bruderhof residents, Jordan corresponded with people from the Iona Community in Scotland; the Aaronic order, which was a pacifist organization; members of the Catholic Worker movement including Dorothy Day; and Reba Place Fellowship in Evanston, Illinois.[22]

John and Louise Miller founded Reba Place in 1957. They and a handful of friends and recent college graduates set up a communal living situation in a low-income area of Evanston. They had goals similar to Koinonia Farm, although they chose city living where they could "serve the poor, the alienated, and the disenfranchised."[23] Reba Place members were seeking "to evolve a new church form."[24] The new church model included pooling possessions, communal housing and meals, and common worship, while members held jobs out in the community.[25]

Reba Place members David Gale, John Lehman, and Don Mast heard about the trouble at Koinonia Farm, and went down to help. John Lehman, one of the original members of Reba Place, spent two months in the winter of 1960 at Koinonia, helping to construct a freezer and build a candy kitchen. It was through his efforts that Koinonia was able greatly to expand their mail-order business to include pecan and peanut candies and fruitcakes.[26]

The connection between Reba Place Fellowship and

Koinonia Farm emphasizes the sense of unity and kinship felt by the two groups, based mainly on their similar understandings of the Christian faith and their similar practice of communal living. After Koinonia's long battle with their neighbors, Koinonia members longed for encouragement and support from like-minded Christians.

It is interesting to note that, although Jordan and some of the other Koinonia residents had taken courses in church history at seminary or Bible colleges, there is no evidence that they studied Christian communities from the past. Although they might have received a number of ideas from monastic groups, Anabaptists of the Reformation, or even the many American communal groups from the eighteenth and nineteenth centuries, Koinonia members seem to have relied only upon existing groups. Jordan did not use any examples from the history of the church in his sermons, lectures, or writings.

To further the support and encouragement between Christian communal groups, Koinonia Farm helped sponsor a Summer Fellowship Conference in 1960.[27] Will Wittkamper included this conference report in the Koinonia files:

> A conference meeting of Christian Community Churches, Reba Place, Evanston, Ill.; Forest River, Fordville, N.D.; Peoria Street Community, Chicago, Ill.; Community of the Brethren, Bright, Ontario, Canada; and Koinonia Community, Americus, Georgia, took place on June 10-12, 1960, at Marycrest Farm, Elgin, Illinois.
>
> The program consisted of Bible study in the early morning. The rest of the day was spent in learning to know each other in a face-to-face fellowship and discussing our common basis of life and witness. We're anticipating working and sharing more together.[28]

Although this conference lasted only three days, it greatly encouraged the Koinonia members. Koinonia was the only group that represented the racially torn South, and the other groups were generally of Anabaptist heritage and biblically conservative. Some scholars have drawn parallels between Jordan and Dorothy Day, with their concern for nonviolence and the poor, or between Jordan and Martin Luther King Jr. with their concern for racial reconciliation.[29] However, it appears that Jordan and other Koinonia members felt their closest kinship with small, biblically conservative, Anabaptist communal groups.

Civil Rights

Jordan's views on the civil rights movement have in retrospect been quite controversial. The late 1950s and 1960s was an era marked by civil rights marches, desegregation of the public schools, and the rise of Martin Luther King Jr. and Malcolm X as civil rights leaders. In addition, a number of seemingly small but very significant incidents happened that created an undercurrent of social upheaval by threatening white dominance in the South. On the one hand, Jordan responded to his surroundings by becoming more active on the individual level in resisting the boycotting that was the result of racism. On the other hand, surprisingly, he did not advocate the kind of public, staged resistance to racism that the civil rights activists were instigating.

Jordan's ambivalence toward the larger civil rights movement was puzzling to many who visited Koinonia Farm. The 1960s were a time of great student activism, and visitors to the farm expected to find energetic discussions about sit-ins, marches, and other activist forms of promoting civil rights. Worldwide, Gandhi's earlier methods of nonviolent resistance had become very well known, and in the South, Martin Luther King Jr. was advocating the use of marches and boycotts to force changes in southern culture.[30] Jordan and other Koinonia members were just beginning to evaluate those approaches to fighting racism.

New Approaches to Nonviolent Resistance

As Koinonia Farm moved from the 1950s into the 1960s, Jordan began to evaluate his passive approach to nonviolent resistance. The entire community was beginning to wonder about its response to the many boycotts that had undermined its farming. Up to that point, the community had responded in a manner Tracy K'Meyer terms "nonresistance."[31] The merchants were confronted once or twice; Jordan often asked them direct questions about their ethical practice in light of Jesus' teachings. After those confrontations, the merchants were no longer pressured.

The theory behind the approach was that the merchants had been given the opportunity to do the right thing, but they were not to be forced. Koinonia members were also concerned that they would push people to respond with violence, and they were weary from the hostility. Because they could not purchase most supplies from the nearby merchants, they continued to secretly arrange for supplies or ask visitors to bring items they needed.

About 1960, after absorbing the approaches of Gandhi and King, the community began to reevaluate their own. They were extremely tired of the boycott, which made daily purchases a complicated process. At the same time, they were beginning to see that they might be enabling the merchants to continue the boycott by letting them off the hook too easily. In addition, the sneaking around and secrecy made the Koinonia members feel that they were being dishonest. Members of Koinonia shifted from not responding to violence to a more active resistance.

That active resistance, although still nonviolent, was characterized by a return to the merchants on a daily basis. Each day, merchants had to renew their boycott as they faced Koinonia members asking to buy or sell products. Although that approach did not affect the boycott until the mid-1960s, Koinonia continued to pursue the more active nonviolent resistance.[32] Even that active approach did not include more public methods such as boycotting in return, picketing, protesting, or marching. The Koinonia practice of nonviolence was characterized more by love than resistance.

Response to Public Activism

To say that Clarence Jordan was not aligned with Martin Luther King Jr. on the issue of civil rights could cause some confusion. During the 1950s, Jordan and other Koinonia members expressed their support and concern for the civil rights work in Montgomery, Alabama, only a few hours drive from Koinonia Farm. At one point, members of Koinonia Farm sent a letter of support to the Montgomery Improvement Association that stated, "We are in complete sympathy with the work you are doing . . . and think of the people in Montgomery often."[33] Many of the southern religious leaders who advocated civil rights asked Jordan to speak at their churches.

Because Koinonia Farm received national coverage while they were boycotted, they became a symbol of integration in the segregated South. Martin Luther King Jr. and Ralph Abernathy thought Jordan's words would encourage Montgomery residents to "take new courage and be inspired to do greater work" in the fight against racism.[34]

It is easy to look back on the events at Koinonia Farm and conclude that Jordan was a champion of the civil rights movement, but he was in fact opposed to some of the actions taken by civil rights leaders. He opposed even nonviolent civil disobedience. He thought marches and picketing only resulted in stirring up more violence. In some cases, he was right. For example, in August 1964 in Albany, Georgia, after a summer of picketing and non-violent protests, demonstrators and police engaged in a violent encounter that led to seventy-seven arrests and injuries on both sides.[35]

He believed that boycotting necessarily involved the same mean and unchristian tactics that Sumter County had deployed against Koinonia Farm. Further, he did not think that staged events, such as groups of African-Americans seeking to be served in segregated coffee shops, would bring about real change. He thought they would only serve to anger the white community. He did, however, think it was perfectly reasonable for anyone, black or white, to go into any public restaurant when they honestly wanted a meal.

For Jordan, the marches, boycotts, and sit-ins seemed artificial and contrived. As K'Meyer notes, "[T]he farm's 'interracial character' was not activism for integration but an offshoot of its loyalty to Jesus."[36]

Clarence's daughter Jan found the Koinonia response to the civil rights movement very frustrating. On the fifti-eth anniversary of the farm, she remembered:

In 1963, the civil rights movement was going strong all over the South. There were sit-ins, beatings, and arrests. We Koinonia kids went to mass meetings on Mondays and Thursday evenings. We sang and registered voters. While Koinonia was a safe place for peace and civil rights people to meet, get away for a few days, receive mail, and just hang out, Koinonia never took part in any demonstrations.[37]

Jan wanted to participate in a march that was coming up, and she appealed to her father to let her go. He replied:

> Jannie, I can go out and kill Sheriff Chappell. I would be "doing" something but what I'd be doing wouldn't be right. You can join in the march. That's your decision. But, if you get arrested, I won't get you out. Call someone else or stay in jail. Because what you're doing isn't right. Now, if you and Lena (a black friend) are in town, and in the course of your time together, it would be natural to go into Walgreen's for a Coke, I not only will come to get you out of jail, but I will go all the way to the Supreme Court to do it because what you're doing is right. Don't go out of your way to cause conflict, but never step aside to avoid it.[38]

Jan wrote, "I never doubted that Daddy would hate to see me stay in jail, but I also know that he really would let me stay there if I took part in a march."[39]

On another occasion, some of the Koinonia residents wanted to boycott a local business because they had racist hiring practices. The Americus Movement, a group that was fighting segregation, had begun the boycott. Jordan refused to support the boycott, stating:

> We've been on the other end of a boycott. I know first-hand how much a boycott hurts. I can't participate in the boycott and be doing unto others as I would not have them do unto me. I've had it done unto me, and I didn't like it one bit.[40]

At one point, Ross Anderson asked Koinonia members to join with the Fellowship of Intentional Communities to bring about world peace through sit-ins and anti-nuclear activities, but Koinonia members again refused.[41] That incident was typical of the tension felt by Koinonia Farm residents in the 1960s.

Visitors

Many visitors came, not because of their Christian faith, but because of the farm's reputation as a place of racial reconciliation and a "happening place to be."[42] The list of visitors who came during the 1960s included "a group of beatniks from Atlanta," a member of the Japanese Parliament, the dean of the Harvard Divinity School, and many young people who were part of the burgeoning hippie movement.[43] Between eight hundred and one thousand people came yearly to stay for short durations of a few hours to a few months.[44] That made the community life interesting but also chaotic and stressful for the members. Dorothy Swisshelm, who had come to Koinonia in 1958, wrote during the 1960s, "We're so busy with housekeeping and making a living we can't give them much attention."[45]

Looking back at Koinonia Farm newsletters, it is easy to see why so many people who were involved in the hippie movement wanted to visit the farm. During the late 1960s, Koinonia residents were selling a number of items that reflected hippie culture through the farm's mail-order business. For example, they sold a variety of patchwork clothing items, macramé wall hangings, dashiki shirts, peasant dresses, and handmade pottery.[46] Anyone who received those mailings might reasonably assume that Koinonia Farm was a hippie commune.

African-American Responses

Local black residents in Sumter County often shunned Koinonia Farm. Rather than seeing Koinonia members as allies, neighboring black families often feared the violence directed at the farm. Although African-Americans had a difficult time in the South, they knew it could be worse, and often tried to distance themselves from the integration that was going on at Koinonia. Several black residents believed the accusations made during the grand jury trial, and they were suspicious of Koinonia Farm's being a communist endeavor. Many African-Americans did not like their place in southern society, but they knew what it was. They were uncomfortable with the shifting societal norms and wondered if some of the shifts would result in setbacks for African-Americans.[47] The result was that neither black nor white residents of Sumter County accepted Koinonia Farm members.

However, a few African-Americans lived on the edges of the farm community or found other ways to support it. During the boycott, black neighbors Doc Champion and Carranza Morgan bought supplies and brought them to Koinonia after dark.[48] At different times African-Americans worked at Koinonia Farms, and some lived on the property, although they were not actually members.

Jordan recounted a conversation he overheard during one of the Ku Klux Klan rallies that summarized the effect Koinonia had on a small group of African-Americans. A handful of black people stood by watching the Klan members during their rally, and a Koinonia member asked about their lack of fear. One of the men responded, "You should know; Koinonia has taught us not to be afraid."[49] That was the response for which Jordan was hoping.

Alma and Mary Jackson and Eddie and Mildred Johnson were a few of the African-Americans who moved to Koinonia with the intention of becoming members. Both couples began the process of membership, but neither couple lasted through the novice meetings. The threats and violence came too close to home, and the adults feared for their children's safety. Alma Jackson said, "I wanted to be there. I liked it there. It was a nice place to live—the right way of living."[50] Jordan had hoped that the community would become truly integrated, but he was not blind to the terrible pressure on the black families. When the Jacksons and the Johnsons left, Koinonia members did not consider it "a true breaking of fellowship, but rather a separation imposed on them from the outside."[51]

Meanwhile, as the violence lessened in the mid-1960s, Koinonia members were able to reestablish friendships with their African-American neighbors. In addition to providing jobs at the pecan plant, Koinonia Farm assisted a number of very poor families. Koinonia members visited elderly couples, distributed the food and clothing that had come in from all over the United States when the boycott was publicized, and participated in a dairy cow distribution project that was sponsored by the Church of the Brethren.[52] Members wrote, "being able to work with these people again without reprisals is a relief and a joy."[53]

The Vietnam War

Jordan maintained his pacifist position as the United States entered the Vietnam War. Anti-war sentiment was much more widespread than during World War II, and Jordan was not singled out as being anti-American. He took the opportunity to write a satire about the government's Selective Service draft process. In the article, written circa 1965, he argued that there should be a draft, but that the minimum age should be 65. He stated that senior citizens "wouldn't even have to be drafted. If we gave them the opportunity they would volunteer in droves" because "no man is more anxious to fight than one who is sure he's too old."[54]

He made certain exceptions to the age limit: the President should be drafted, to improve morale, and the House Un-American Activities Committee since it has "repeatedly demonstrated its uncanny ability to detect with infallible accuracy all shades of communists, com-symps, and fellow travelers."[55] Because many of those soldiers would be retired bankers, politicians, economists, and executives, they would be ready to reconstruct the government and economy of the invaded country:

> In mere weeks after storming the beaches, all these mighty architects of the American Dream, these wrinkled but wise GIs, would transform alien lands into prosperous territories ready for statehood. With prospects of such affluent bliss, most countries would actually invite us to invade them. . . . It might be necessary to have a war waiting list.[56]

Jordan preached against the Vietnam War and the draft, and his son Jim took his words to heart, registering as a conscientious objector and doing alternative service.[57]

Jimmy Carter and Koinonia Farm

Since Americus is quite close to Plains, Georgia, and some of the Koinonia children attended school in Plains, many have wondered to what extent former United States President Jimmy Carter was aware of or involved with Koinonia Farm.

In his spiritual autobiography *Living Faith*, Jimmy Carter told of being raised by a father who saw racism as a normal part of life in the South and a mother who questioned racist behaviors and fought them in her own personal ways. "Daddy accepted the racial segregation of the South as a way of life," Carter wrote, and "Mama refused to recognize the strict racial segregation of our south Georgia community and throughout her life was considered by some of our neighbors somewhat strange concerning this issue."[58] Carter's father participated in the beginnings of the boycott of Koinonia Farm in the 1950s, but he died in 1953.

Carter admitted that he did not see a problem with the racist attitudes and business practices in the South until he went into the military. "It was only after I entered the Navy in my late teens," Carter wrote, "that I came to understand that black and white people should be treated with complete equality."[59] During the early years of Koinonia Farm, Carter was too young to be involved and later he was away from Georgia in the military. He returned to rural Georgia after he left the Navy in 1953, and there he was confronted with a new pressure to conform to racist practices.

Carter began a farm supply business, and in 1955 he was pressured by a group of white men from the Plains area who wanted Carter to join the White Citizens' Council. Carter refused, which resulted in a boycott of his business by some local people.[60] The boycotting lessened in the late 1950s and early 1960s, but in 1965 Carter's business was again subject to a boycott. The local John Birch Society members began spreading rumors that the Carters were Communists, although Carter had been a Georgia state senator for three years, and his anti-communistic political views were known to all.[61]

Carter was aware of the difficulties, violence, and boycotting at Koinonia Farm. He understood the stress of being boycotted through personal experience. In the early 1960s when Koinonia Farm was beginning its pecan and peanut business, Carter and his family sold Koinonia

Farm seed peanuts and processed the crop in their peanut shelling plant.[62] In addition, as a member of the Plains Board of Education, Carter worked to allow the Koinonia children to attend school in the Plains district when the Americus schools rejected them. In 1963, Dorothy Swisshelm wrote to Carter, telling of the hard times that Koinonia Farm endured. Carter had been a state senator for a year, and Dorothy hoped that he would intervene to stop the boycotting and violence.

Carter did not intervene in any noticeable way at that time, but it is clear from his writing in *Living Faith* that Carter later admired Koinonia Farm. When giving a very brief history of Koinonia Partners, Carter called Clarence Jordan and the other Koinonia members in the early years "a few dedicated and courageous white Christians."[65] Carter was reacquainted with Koinonia Partners through his contact with Habitat for Humanity, and he commented that workers at both groups "attempt to demonstrate their own religious faith by serving the poor and needy in an often sacrificial way."[66] Carter's understanding of the goals and aims of Koinonia residents and the centrality of their faith serves to support the thesis of this book. Jimmy Carter, too, has seen that Koinonia's actions came out of its theology.

A Different Entity?

Because of the hostility, violence, and economic boycott imposed on Koinonia Farm, it would perhaps not be surprising for the original vision to have been compromised. Perhaps Koinonia Farm was questioning its position on racial integration. Perhaps even individual Koinonia members came out of the violence and persecution questioning their own approach to race relations. As mentioned, some members wondered whether they ought to be more assertive, while others wondered whether they had been too proactive in their approach. Were they standing for what was right, or were they aggravating an already violent situation?

It is true that many Koinonia community programs, such as vacation Bible school, ended and that the focus of the agricultural side of the farm shifted from local to mail-order business. However, the original intent of that communal experiment was not to improve race relations, but to live out primitive Christianity.

Jordan looked at the Gospels and Acts and tried to see what New Testament Christianity might look like. He then began the farming community, which was not founded on a platform of interracialism, or nonviolence, or communal living, in and of themselves. He began the community after studying Jesus' teaching and by trying to live an authentic Christian life—a communal life of nonviolence and racial harmony. However, those were results of acting out his theology, not the cornerstones of his movement.

Koinonia Farm may have looked different, because some of the ministries and the approaches to farming changed, but the farm did not become a different entity. Members still stood by their understanding of living out the kingdom of God.

A New Era

Although Koinonia Farm was not becoming a new entity, it was experiencing some alterations in its outward approach to community and ministry. Clarence Jordan continued to develop Koinonia Farm based on his understanding of the Sermon on the Mount and Acts 2, but he realized that some organizational changes needed to be made.

By the mid-1960s, Jordan was completely out of energy, and the community was struggling to find its identity in the shifting ideals of that decade. The pecan business was doing well though, and he wanted to have more time to travel and speak around the country. His Cotton Patch versions of the New Testament letters were very popular, and Jordan wanted to use them as a springboard for talking about his idea of God's kingdom.

Millard and Linda Fuller decided to visit Koinonia Farm during that time. Millard Fuller was a young millionaire from Alabama who had decided that his money-oriented life was empty. He sold his boat, house, and some of his cars, and took his family on a road trip. Millard and Linda were friends with a pastor from Birmingham who was staying at Koinonia Farm. They decided to visit him there, hoping to chat, have lunch, and be on their way. Millard began talking with Clarence during that lunch, and his family stayed for a month. After working in Mississippi for a short time, the Fullers went back to Koinonia Farm and stayed for five years.[67]

Millard was the sort of person who naturally attracts money, and he was also very good at putting ideas into action on a large scale. He and Jordan began to brainstorm about new ways of living out the goals of Koinonia Farm. They were particularly interested in helping the poor in Sumter County have better housing. As Fuller describes it:

> Clarence Jordan was a great dreamer. He and I used to have a grand time of sitting together in his little study out in the middle of the field, and dreaming and talking and planning and thinking about this whole idea. We said we would like to just get rid of all these shacks in Sumter County, just wipe 'em away from the county.[68]

In 1968, Jordan wrote a letter to the friends and supporters of Koinonia Farm, describing the new direction he intended to pursue:

For several years it has been clear that Koinonia stands at the end of an era or perhaps of its existence. Its goals and methods, which were logical and effective in the 1940s and 50s, seem no longer relative to an age that is undergoing vast and rapid changes. An integrated Christian community was a very practical vehicle through which to witness to a segregated society a decade ago, but now it is too slow, too weak, not aggressive enough. Its lack of mobility gives it the appearance of a house on the bank of a river as the rushing torrents of history swirl by.

The obvious answer was to call it quits. The group had already dwindled to a mere handful—two families, to be exact. About a year ago, Florence and I decided that we would seek other directions, and friends extended invitations to join faculties, to pastor churches, to be this-and-that-in-residence, etc.

But somehow nothing seemed to click. Perhaps I was suffering from "battle fatigue." It was as though I were living in a spiritual vacuum. No joy, no excitement, no sense of mission.

In this state of torpor, I got a very brief note from Millard Fuller, whom I had met in December of 1965 when he and his family stopped at Koinonia to visit for a half-hour with his friend Al Henry. As the half-hour stretched into a day and finally into a month, we learned that this was a time of deep spiritual crisis for Millard and his wife, Linda, and that both had reached the brink of destruction. Millard had become a "money addict" and was more enslaved to it than any alcoholic to his bottle. He has already become a millionaire and was reaching for more.

But God reached for him, turned him around, and gave him the wisdom to do what even the rich young ruler in the Bible wouldn't do—"Go, sell what thou hast and give it to the poor, and come, follow me."

During his month here, Millard transacted by phone much of the business necessary to liquidate his assets in Montgomery, Alabama, and to distribute them to charitable purposes. Being a white native of Alabama, Millard wanted to express his discipleship to Christ in service to blacks. He got a job raising money for Tougaloo College, a Negro school near Jackson, Mississippi. In this he was both happy and successful.

His note to me in May of this year was brief and direct. "I have just resigned my job with Tougaloo. What have you got up your sleeve?"

Nothing up my sleeve or in my head or heart, I'm blank.

But wait a minute. Does God have something up *his* sleeve—for both of us? I got on the phone and called Millard at his New York office. Could God be trying to say something to us, to accomplish some purpose through us?

We decided to get together at once and discuss it. I would be preaching in a few days at the Oakhurst Baptist Church in Atlanta, and we decided to meet there. At the end of a long day of discussion and prayer, both of us were convinced that God had given a radically new direction to our lives.

We still cannot fully articulate this leading of God's Spirit. But we have the deep feeling that modern man's greatest problems stem from his loss of any sense of meaningful participation with God in his purposes for mankind. For most people God really and truly is dead, stone dead.

With no upward reach, no sense of partnership with God, man has chosen to be a loner, trying to solve on his own, but always in deep frustration and desperation, crushing problems which increasingly threaten to destroy him. But from bitter experience, beginning at the Tower of Babel, we should know by now that "unless the Lord builds the house, those who build it labor in vain."

The church has been saying this all along—without believing its own message. So it has thrown up its hands and joined the multitudes who look to the government for salvation. But even with billions of dollars at its disposal, government cannot give man a God-dimension to his life. It is inherently incapable of reaching the inner recesses of his being, which must be touched if life on this planet is to be even passingly tolerable.

It has also become clear to us that as man has lost his identity with God he has lost it with his fellowman. We compete with one another fiercely; we even want to kill human beings for whom Christ died. Our cities provide us anonymity, not community. Instead of partners, we are aliens and strangers.

As a result, the poor are being driven from rural areas; frustrated, angry masses huddle in the cities; suburbanites walk in fear; the chasm between blacks and whites grows wider; war hysteria invades every part of the earth.

We must have a new spirit—a spirit of partnership with one another.

But how does a dream become deed and a vision reality? Can lofty speculation be transformed into practical, hard-hosed action?

In mid-August of 1968, we called together fifteen spiritually sensitive and socially aware men of God for a four-day session of seeking, thinking, talking about these questions. They were businessmen, politicians, writers, ministers, freelancers—all with a deep compassion for their fellowmen. From this conference emerged a course of action which we shall call Koinonia Partners. It will have three prongs: (1) communication, (2) instruction, (3) application.

1. By *communication* we mean the sowing of the seed, the spreading of the radical ideas of the gospel message; the call to faith in God and the reshaping and restructuring of our lives around his will and purpose. It means "to preach good news to the poor, to proclaim release to the captives and recovering of sight to the blind, to set at liberty those who are oppressed."

To do this we will use every available means of modern communication. We will travel and speak extensively across the land and throughout the world. We will make tapes, records, and films, publish books, and circulate literature in every way possible. Already a good start has been made in this direction, but it will be greatly intensified.

2. By *instruction* we mean the constant teaching and training of the "partners" to enable them to become more effective and mature. There will be traveling "discipleship schools" to follow up and conserve the results of the speaking and communicating, to keep alive the new spirit, to strengthen and encourage. The first such school is already scheduled for early January of 1969.

3. *Application*, in its initial stages, will consist of *partnership industries, partnership farming,* and *partnership housing.* These will be implemented through a Fund for Humanity.

What the poor need is not charity but capital, not caseworkers but co-workers. And what the rich need is a wise, honorable and just way of divesting themselves of their overabundance. The Fund for Humanity will meet both of these needs.

Money for the Fund will come from shared gifts by those who feel that they have more than they need, from non-interest-bearing loans from those who cannot afford to make the gift but who do want to provide working capital for the disinherited, and from the voluntarily shared profits from the partnership industries, farms, and houses. As a starter, it has been agreed to transfer all of Koinonia Farm's assets of about $250,000 to the Fund. Other gifts are already beginning to come in.

The Fund will give away no money. It is not a handout. It will provide capital for the partnership enterprises.

The first enterprise to be launched is *partnership farming.* Under this plan all land will be held in trust by the Fund for Humanity, but will be used by the partners free of charge. Thus, usership will replace ownership. This can be done because the Fund's capital has been provided by those who care, and there is no need to pay interest on it.

The partners will be strongly encouraged, though not required, to contribute as liberally as possible to the Fund so as to keep enlarging it and making more capital available to others. As Jesus put it, "You have received it as a gift, so share it as a gift." If the partners have the right spirit (and I cannot see how this or any system can work without that) and there should be growing numbers—which it seems reasonable to predict—the Fund will be self-generative and ever-expanding.

The same principles will be applied to *partnership industries.* We already have a fairly flourishing pecan-shelling plant, fruitcake bakery, candy kitchen, and mail-order business. Once again, partners will operate these ventures with no capital outlay in the beginning and never any rent or interest.

Partnership housing is concerned with the idea that the urban ghetto is to a considerable extent the product of rural displacement. People don't move to the city unless life in the country has become intolerable; they do not voluntarily choose the degrading life in the big city slums. If land in the country is available on which to build a decent house, and if they can get jobs nearby to support their families, they'll stay put.

So we have recently laid off 42 half-acre home sites and are making them available to displaced rural families. Four acres in the center are being reserved as a community park and recreational area. The Fund for Humanity will put up a four-bedroom house with bath, kitchen and living room, and this will be sold to a family over a twenty-year period with no interest, only a small monthly administration charge. Thus the cost will be about half the usual financing, and for a poor person this can be the difference between owning a house and not owning one. The interest forces him to pay for two houses but he gets only one.

As with farming and industries, the partner family will gradually free the initial capital to build houses for others and will be encouraged to share at least a part of their savings on interest with the Fund for Humanity. Even as all are benefited, so should all share. If, as Jesus says, "It is more blessed to give than to get," then even the poorest should not be denied the extra blessedness of giving.

Perhaps I have now given you at least some understanding of Koinonia Partners and the new direction for my own life. I would like to encourage each of you to rethink your life and make whatever adjustments you feel necessary to bring it into line with the will of God.

Augustine once said, "He who possesses a surplus possesses the goods of others." That's a polite way of saying that anybody who has too much is a thief. If you are a "thief," perhaps you should set a reasonable living standard for your family and restore the "stolen goods" to humanity, either through the Fund or by some other suitable means. Some of you may wish to join us and seek the new life of partnership with God and man.

Yours in faith and expectation,
Clarence Jordan[69]

Jordan, along with Millard Fuller, began to work out this idea of partnership. The name of the community was changed to Koinonia Partners, and a number of ministries were started. A daycare and nursery school were begun, and a non-profit housing development for the poor was started. It is easy to see the beginnings of what would develop into Habitat for Humanity in the housing developments and Fund for Humanity that were put into effect. Not all the ideas outlined in the statement were brought to fruition, but many were. Koinonia Partners still included the pecan and peanut farming and processing; they remain its main sources of income today.

✳ ✳ ✳

The actions and teachings that characterized Clarence Jordan and Koinonia Farm during the 1960s continued to undergird the idea that the farm was established for theological reasons and was intended as a demonstration plot for God's kingdom. Koinonia was not locked into one particular model of developing community or racial reconciliation. It could and did change its ways of farming, becoming more of a business. It also changed its ways of reaching out to bridge the gap between blacks and whites, by beginning a housing program and a daycare center rather than continuing to sponsor agricultural education. Meanwhile, Jordan's response to the civil rights movement was ambivalent, although he was certainly advocating equality.

Although Jordan and other Koinonia members were willing to change their methods of approaching various issues, their commitment to their understanding of the kingdom of God remained. Unlike some communal groups, Koinonia Farm was not left behind by progress. It adapted, and yet the core message of living out the

Gospel as they understood it held the struggling group together.

Even as Jordan and Fuller reinvented Koinonia Farm as Koinonia Partners, their basic commitment was to live in the way to which they believed Jesus was calling them and calling all Christians. When Koinonia members arranged for a conference of people who were like-minded, they chose other communal groups who were theologically or spiritually driven. Looking at his interests, actions, and priorities, it is clear that Jordan was moved by his understanding of Christianity and that his views on race, nonviolence, and community flowed from his theology.

9

The Cotton Patch Versions

Jordan preached using only a few notes and his Greek New Testament, translating into the Georgia dialect as he went. As early as 1955, his supporters were asking him to write down his own personal translations of the New Testament. After hearing about Rock and Andy Johnson and Mary Davidson in his sermons, people wanted to see what Jordan's version would look like in a written translation. Russ Berry, a Sunday school teacher at Grant Park Baptist Church in Portland, Oregon, asked him, "Have you done a complete translation of the entire New Testament? If so, is it available?"[1]

Jordan's version of sections of the New Testament became better known as he preached around the country, and not just among church groups. In the spring of 1960, James S. Best of the Associated Press contacted him about writing "a book on the Greek Testament translated freely for today."[2]

Jordan decided to create what he called "cotton patch" versions of the books of the New Testament. With Jordan's emphasis on Jesus and the Sermon on the Mount, one might expect that he would begin with Matthew or at least one of the Gospels, but he began with Hebrews and James.[3] That makes sense, because he was writing for a primarily Christian audience. He wanted to find biblical texts that pushed his readers to act, to be involved, and to do good works. Hebrews, with its emphasis on running the race to the end, and James, with its claim that faith without works is dead, were just what Jordan wanted.[4] There were plenty of people in his audiences and also in his neighborhood who would claim to be Christians, but he wanted to challenge those people to act as they believed.

In the Translator's Notes for Hebrews and the general epistles, Jordan gives his reason for choosing those texts. He says that those writings "come from some of the earliest partners in the faith of Jesus Christ and sparkle with keen insight and spiritual perception."[5] He liked the fact that those letters "abound in compassion, love, encouragement, and hope."[6] He wanted his readers to be gripped with a passion for living out their faith, and he thought those letters would provide the "fiery zeal" that would warn them of "the perils of indifference and lukewarmness."[7] Jordan hoped the modern paraphrases would bring the biblical texts into the twentieth century in such a way as to incite people to action.

Although later Cotton Patch versions became well known for the views on race that they included, the first translations were a simpler attempt to update the texts. In later works, Jordan translated the tension between Jews and Gentiles into the tension between blacks and whites. The setting is Georgia, and he used the names of Georgia cities. However, in the early translations, he kept the biblical place names Jerusalem, Mount Sinai, and Egypt, and he retained the Jew and Gentile distinction. Sometimes, but not consistently, Jewish leaders were translated as clergymen.[8] In many ways, the early Cotton Patch versions were as tied to the first century as to the twentieth. What made them unique was the use of south

Georgia language. Here is an example from Hebrews 12:1-3:

> Now here's where we come in. Surrounded by such a cloud of veterans of the faith, let's strip off all heavy and tight-fitting clothes and run with endurance the race stretching out before us. Let's keep our eyes fixed on Jesus, the founder and guiding spirit of our way of life. In place of joy that stretched out before him, he took on a cross, without hesitating one second to consider the disgrace involved.[9]

As Jordan translated James, he began to include some of his ideas about racial reconciliation, although only to a small degree. James 2:8-9 is an example of how he began incorporating ideas about race: "So if you observe the Scripture's finest law—'Love your neighbor as yourself'—you're doing all right. But if you segregate, you commit a sin, and stand convicted under the law as a violator."[10]

One of the best known phrases from the Cotton Patch versions comes from Jordan's translation of Hebrews 11:1: "Now faith is the turning of dreams into deeds; it is betting your life on the unseen realities."[11] The phrase "turning dreams into deeds" became even better known when Henlee Barnette used it as the subtitle for his book on Jordan's ethics.[12] Jordan had made the Bible clearer for the lay people in his community and in the churches where he preached. His later versions, though, were much more radical, and therefore more controversial.

Jordan's Later Intent

After Jordan had finished translating Paul's letters, he realized he wanted to write a defense of his version, which he included in the preface to *The Cotton Patch*

Version of Paul's Epistles.[13] In those texts, he had taken a more revolutionary approach to translating. He made a stronger statement against racism and he brought the texts closer to the twentieth century.

He listed three intentions of his new style of translating, the first being the problem of cultural distance. He complained that modern translations "still have left us stranded in some faraway land in the long-distant past."[14] Calling his projects *versions* rather than *translations,* he said he wanted people to be participants in the Christian faith. He tried to make that possible by translating "not only the words, but [also] the events."[15] Jordan wanted the words to be alive and relevant for twentieth-century America.

Second, he wanted the Scriptures to be "taken out of the classroom and stained-glass sanctuary and put out under God's skies where people are toiling and crying and wondering."[16] He did not want the letters of Paul to be formal or academic, but to be seen as letters written to simple, humble people.[17] Jordan's third reason flowed from the second. He wanted the "little people of great faith," whom he found in rural church pews and out working in their fields, to understand Jesus' message in their own words.[18]

Jordan then described his theory of translation in more detail. He stated that he was trying to translate the ideas, not the words. He was concerned that often the "actual words convey the wrong impression to the modern hearer."[19] Given that he was working, not only with two languages that were separated by a huge time gap, but also with "the barriers of culture and space," Jordan admitted that it was hard to find present-day equivalents.[20] For example, he translated the word crucifixion as lynching. He thought the ideas of violence, indignity, stigma, and defeat were best conveyed to a southern audience by the term lynching, but he admitted that lynchings lacked the trial and legal condemnation that characterized Jesus' crucifixion.[21]

The Racial Focus

Perhaps the most important decision that Jordan made in his Cotton Patch versions was to translate *Jew* and *Gentile* (and *Pharisee* and *sinner*) as *white man* and *Negro*.[22] In considering his decision, he asked, "In the southern context, is there any other alternative?"[23]

When Jordan translated Romans, which he titled "The Letter to the Christians in Washington," he handled Paul's discussion in Romans 9 of whether or not Gentiles are full and true believers in this way:

> As a Christian who doesn't lie and whose conscience is examined by the Holy Spirit, I'm telling you the honest truth: In my heart there is great grief and steady pain. For I would be willing to sacrifice even my own life in Christ for the sake of my native white American Protestant brethren. They are "good white folks"; they are "saved"; they have prestige; they have the Bible; they have a denominational program; they have worship services and Sunday schools; they have theological doctrines and are staunch supporters of Christ himself. And God, who is over them all, is unceasingly magnified. So be it. But it was not for the likes of this that the word of God has come raining down. For not all Protestants are Protestants, and not all "good white folks" are *good* white folks. (Rom. 9:1-7)[24]

Later, in Romans 9:27, Jordan equated the Jewish establishment with the white religious establishment. He wrote, "And Isaiah cries out regarding white American Protestants, 'Even though the WAPs [white American

Protestants] outnumber the sand of the seas, it's those that are left that shall be saved.'"[25] Jordan explained his translation in a footnote, stating that white American Protestants were a legitimate translation of the people of Israel because Israel "refers to Judaism both racially and religiously."[26] When translating Romans, one of his early Pauline translations, he identified the Jews with white people, but he did not identify the Gentiles with blacks. Rather, in that letter he called the Gentiles outsiders: presumably anyone who was not white and Protestant and American.[27] By the time he translated Galatians and Ephesians, he chose to make a more direct statement by translating Gentile as black or Negro.[28]

Translation Problems

In trying to create a version in which racial tension was the main conflict, Jordan sometimes painted himself into a theological corner. For example, in his translation of Galatians, which he titled "The Letter to the Churches of the Georgia Convention," Jordan compared the problems between Jews and Gentiles and those experienced by blacks and whites. The difficulty is in the translation of Galatians 3:28-29:

> No more is one a white man and another a Negro; no more is one a slave and the other a free man; no longer is one a male and the other a female. For you *all* are as *one* in Christ Jesus. And if you are Christ's men, then you are true "white men," noble heirs of a *spiritual* heritage.[29]

The problem is that African-Americans in general do not want to be "true white men." The analogy has broken down, but Jordan was forced by his translation choices to push his theology in a way that fit the Jews as the people of God but does not fit southern white heritage.

Jordan's version of the third chapter of Ephesians is much closer to his intent, described in the introduction, of choosing to replace *Jew and Gentile* with *white and black.* In Ephesians, titled "The Letter to the Christians in Birmingham," he translated Ephesians 3:6 as "The secret is that the Negroes are fellow partners and equal members, co-sharers in the privileges of the gospel of Jesus Christ."[30] His point in making the comparison between the Gentiles and African-Americans was to show the equivalence between the two races (and presumably the equality of all races), and therefore to encourage local churches to welcome people of all races as a witness of the gospel.

Acts

Jordan continued to translate *Jews* as *white American Protestants* in his version of Acts, which he titled "Happenings."[31] By that time, he brought more direct critiques of southern racism into his translations. For example, in translating Acts 9:28-9, the early years after Saul's conversion, Jordan used this description: "So he [Saul] stayed with them, operating in and out of Atlanta, fearlessly bearing the name of the Lord, and getting into discussions and debates with the Klan."[32] In that case, Jordan translated *Hellenistic Jews* as *the Klan*, a rather startling and ironic translation choice considering the attitude of Klansmen toward Jews.

With regard to race, the most significant passage from Acts is the account of Peter's vision in Acts 10. Peter, known as Rock, is waiting for lunch when he sees a vision:

While the folks were fixing lunch, Rock fell into a trance, and he saw a hole in the sky and an outfit like a big four-cornered tablecloth being let down to the ground. In it were all kinds of meat, seafood, and fowl. About that time he heard somebody call, "Come on, Rock, sit down and let's eat!" But Rock said, "Oh, no, sir. I've never eaten anything that was inferior or not kosher." The voice said once, and then repeated, "If God makes something kosher, don't you treat it as dirty." This was said a third time, and then the whole outfit was pulled back up into the sky.[33]

Meanwhile, a black military man named Captain Cornwall received a vision to send for Rock. Rock went to Captain Cornwall's home and said to him,

Y'all understand how uncustomary it is for a white man to socialize or stay with people of a different race, don't you? All right, but as for me, God has made it plain as day to me that I'm never to think of any man as inferior or no good. That's why I came without batting an eye when I was sent for. . . .

I am convinced beyond any doubt . . . that God pays no attention to a man's skin. Regardless of his race, the man who respects God and practices justice is welcomed by him. This point was made clear to the white people when the good news of peace through Jesus Christ was preached. He indeed is Lord of *all* people.[34]

Jordan was still trying to juggle first-century conflicts with twentieth-century ones. He left the idea of food being kosher in his translation. Kosher fit the original Jewish context, but it did not make sense in modern southern culture. In addition, in one case, he used the parallel between first-century Judaism and the Jews of the Holocaust. In Acts 18, Jordan updated Aquila and Priscilla in this way:

There he [Paul] met a Jew named Abrams, a native of
Bavaria, with his wife, Priscilla, who had come to this
country from Germany when Hitler ran all the Jews out
of Berlin. Paul went over to their house and stayed with
them, and since they had the same trade, they worked
together. (They were electricians by trade.) Every Sunday
he held a discussion at the church to which he invited
both whites and blacks.[35]

As if Jordan's critics were not already scandalized, in that
translation he put whites, blacks, and Jews all in one
church! It is easy to see why those later Cotton Patch
translations both gained support for Koinonia Farm and
provided fuel for opposition.

The Gospels
By the time Jordan had translated the Gospels, he had
stopped using the *white American Protestant* translation
for *Jews* and was using only *white*. He also consistently
translated *Gentile* as *Negro*. He used many more locations
in Georgia and used more colloquial language than ever.
His translation of Luke 4:25-27 illustrated those changes:

And I'm telling you straight, there were a lot of white
widows in Georgia during the time of Elijah, when the
skies were locked up for three years and six months, and
there was a great drought everywhere, but Elijah didn't
stay with any of them. Instead, he stayed with a Negro
woman over in Terrell County. And there were a lot of
sick white people during the time of the great preacher
Elisha, but he didn't heal any of them—only Naaman the
African.[36]

That also illustrates Jordan's usual retention of the Old
Testament names as found in English translations,

although he had enjoyed creating nicknames for New Testament characters.

Two of Jesus' parables appear to have been Jordan's favorites. He went back to them again and again in his preaching and lectures. They are known as the parable of the prodigal son and the parable of the good Samaritan. It has been seen (chapter 7) how the prodigal son parable was one of the sermon topics Jordan often chose—using his interesting interpretive quirk of combining that story with the story of the man possessed by Legion. The good Samaritan (Luke 10:25-37) became an oft-quoted parable because it hits at the heart of racism:

> One day a teacher of an adult Bible class got up and tested him with this question: "Doctor, what does one do to be saved?"
>
> Jesus replied, "What does the Bible say? How do you interpret it?"
>
> The teacher answered, "Love the Lord your God with all your heart and with all your soul and with all your physical strength and with all your mind; and love your neighbor as yourself."
>
> "That is correct," answered Jesus. "Make a habit of this and you'll be saved."
>
> But the Sunday school teacher, trying to save face, asked, "But . . . er . . . but . . . just who *is* my neighbor?"
>
> Then Jesus laid into him and said, "A man was going from Atlanta to Albany and some gangsters held him up. When they had robbed him of his wallet and brand-new suit, they beat him up and drove off in his car, leaving him unconscious on the shoulder of the highway.
>
> "Now it just so happened that a white preacher was going down that same highway. When he saw the fellow, he stepped on the gas and went scooting by." (Jordan's original footnote was: "His homiletical mind probably

made the following outline: 1. I do not know the man. 2. I do not wish to get involved in any court proceedings. 3. I don't want to get blood on my new upholstering. 4. the man's lack of proper clothing would embarrass me upon my arrival in town. 5. And finally, brethren, a minister must never be late for worship services.")[37]

"Shortly afterwards a white gospel song leader came down the road, and when he saw what had happened, he too stepped on the gas." (Jordan's footnote: "What his thoughts were we'll never know, but as he whizzed past, he may have been whistling, 'Brighten the corner where you are.'")[38]

"Then a black man traveling that way came upon the fellow, and what he saw moved him to tears. He stopped and bound up his wounds as best he could, drew some water from his water jug to wipe away the blood and then laid him on the back seat." (Jordan's footnote: "All the while his thoughts may have been along this line: 'Somebody's robbed you; yeah, I know about that, I been robbed, too. And they done beat you up bad; I know, I been beat up, too. And everybody just go right on by and leave you laying there hurting. Yeah, I know. They pass me by, too.'")[39] He drove into Albany and took him to the hospital and said to the nurse, 'You all take good care of this white man I found on the highway. Here's the only two dollars I got, but you all keep account of what he owes, and if he can't pay it, I'll settle up with you when I make a payday.'

"Now if you had been the man held up by the gangsters, which of these three—the white preacher, the white song leader, or the black man—would you consider to have been the neighbor?

The teacher of the adult Bible class said, "Why, of course, the nig—I mean, er . . . well, er . . . the one who treated me kindly."

Jesus said, "Well, then *you* get going and start living like that!"[40] Jordan obviously set the scene so that racist white people were equated with the Pharisees and Jewish leaders and the African-Americans and sympathetic white people with the Gentiles and sinners. To make sure the reader got the point, Jordan used blunt words at the beginning of Luke 15:

> Now all the "nigger-lovers" and black people were gathering around him [Jesus] to listen. And the white church people and Sunday school teachers were raising cain, saying, "This fellow associates with black people and eats with them."[41]

It is no wonder Jordan irritated local church people. It could hardly be any clearer—for him, it was the white church people and Sunday school teachers who were against Jesus.

In addition to pointing his readers to the racial issues, Jordan also made his translations fun to read. It is enjoyable to visualize this version of the story of John the Baptist from Luke 3:

> Now during the fifteenth year of Tiberius as President, while Pontius Pilate was governor of Georgia, and Herod was governor of Alabama, his brother Philip being governor of Mississippi, and Lysanias still holding out over Arkansas; while Annas and Caiaphas were co-presidents of the Southern Baptist Convention, the word of God came to Zack's boy, John, down on the farm.
>
> This guy John was dressed in blue jeans and a leather jacket, and he was living on corn bread and collard greens. Folks were coming to him from Atlanta and all over north Georgia and the backwater of the Chattahoochee.[42] And as they owned up to their crooked ways, he dipped them in the Chattahoochee.

Jesus was born in Gainsville and wrapped in an apple box. His family fled to Mexico, and the religious center was Atlanta.[43] Part of the enjoyment of reading Jordan's versions is in seeing how cleverly he transforms elements of the familiar texts.

Community and Nonviolence

Although certainly the Cotton Patch versions are known mostly for their commentary on racism in the South, Jordan also emphasized other aspects of the kingdom of God. In particular, his ideas on community and communal living and his beliefs on pacifism and nonviolence were also evident. Communal ownership of property and a communal noon meal characterized Koinonia Farm. In addition, Koinonia members were expected to open their homes in hospitality whenever there were guests or visitors. Koinonia Farm was also characterized by its pacifist stance. Jordan's translations of key texts made his views on those subjects plain.

An important Scripture passage for Jordan in his understanding of community was Acts 2:42-46. His Cotton Patch version reads:

They [the believers] were all bound together by the officers' instruction and by the sense of community, by the common meal and the prayers. A great reverence came over everybody, while many amazing and instructive things were done by the officers. The whole company of believers stuck together and held all things common. They were selling their goods and belongings, and dividing them among the group on the basis of one's need. Knit together with singleness of purpose they gathered at the church every day, and as they ate the common meal from house to house they had a joyful and humble spirit, praising God and showing overflowing kindness toward everybody.[44]

Jordan believed that was a description of the early church, and he expected modern Christians to follow its model.

One of the slightly puzzling aspects of the Cotton Patch versions is the use of military imagery. Jordan translated a number of words and phrases that were not originally military terms in Greek into metaphors relating to war and military service. He may have used some of them because they were so much a part of the 1960s culture. For example, when speaking of the Gentiles—in his translation the WAPs—he wrote, "God's selective service act classifies them as 'beloved sons' on account of their heritage."[45] He translated Isaiah 13:19 as it was found in Romans 9:29 to read, "If the Lord of peace had not left us a germ of life, we would have wound up like Hiroshima, and would have been treated like Nagasaki."[46] That last phrase did not use war in a positive light, but it is interesting that Jordan the pacifist used war imagery at all.

The God Movement

In the Gospels and Acts, Jordan translated the kingdom of God into the God movement.[47] He seemed to have done that to connect with the emerging hippie movement and to tap into civil rights language. Jesus was the founder of the God movement, the main lessons of which were found in the Sermon on the Mount. Talk of a God movement made the rural southerners rather nervous, as it sounded too radical and potentially communistic. It was, however, quite appealing to the thousands of hippies and civil rights advocates who were drawn to Koinonia Farm because of communal living and racial reconciliation. Perhaps Jordan found the language to have too much cultural baggage because he used the phrase less in Matthew than in Luke and Acts, although Matthew uses the kingdom of God much more often than Luke.

Reviews and Critiques

The Cotton Patch versions received mixed reviews. Most people were drawn to what Ray Martens called "the charm of the translation," which he attributed to a clever and humorous use of idioms and colloquial language.[48] Martens was particularly pleased with Jordan's "way of using the turn of a phrase to take the Scriptures out of the classroom and stained glass sanctuary and put them out under God's skies, specifically southern skies."[49] Reviewer Louis Martyn thought that Jordan had done an excellent job of making a culturally relevant translation and that he had "kept faith with these early writers" by using his approach.[50]

However, there have been some critics of the Cotton Patch versions. The general criticism was that Jordan was making very specific modern interpretations of the biblical texts and presenting them as translations. Jordan was aware of the problem, and he addressed it by avoiding the term *translation* and claiming only that they were *versions* of the Scriptures.

One important criticism was that Jordan's translation of Jew and Gentile into white and black made, not only social and racial changes, but also significant theological changes. Ray Martens commented:

The major themes of Paul and his carefully devised arguments and explanations with regard to the core of the Christian faith lose their punch too frequently in this translation. Some of the great classic chapters of Romans on grace and justification are only shadows of their former selves. The bold absolutes and universals of the letter to the Galatians, now addressed to the Georgia Convention, have been narrowed severely.[51]

Certainly the clarity of biblical history, particularly as it impacted the development of the nation of Israel and the beginning of the church, was also at stake.

Another criticism was that the Cotton Patch versions were distinctly rural and southern, and therefore did not always make sense in other American cultural settings. Louis Martyn praised Jordan for writing versions that spoke to "the backwoods and crossroads gas stations of Georgia," but he realized there would be a cultural gap between the Cotton Patch versions and "urban ghetto" readers.[52]

✳ ✳ ✳

Throughout this work, we have seen how Jordan attempted to live out his theology of the kingdom of God. In his book *Sermon on the Mount* and in his sermons, he articulated some of his ideas about the kingdom. In his Cotton Patch versions, his interpretation of many New Testament passages and their application to rural Georgia in the 1950s and 60s were made clear.

Because of his translation choices emphasizing racial issues, Jordan's reputation as a civil rights leader mushroomed. Ironically, although they were versions of the biblical texts, his Christian faith was often treated as less important by the media, by some of his advocates, and by many of his opponents. However, it must be remembered that he did not choose to write civil rights speeches. He was translating the biblical texts, which he considered to be the primary source of Jesus' teaching.

When Jordan first began the Cotton Patch versions, his

translations stayed very close to the original Greek. He simply translated names and phrases into southern dialect. In translating his second book, James, he began to add his interpretation of the biblical text with reference to the racial conflict of southern Georgia. Throughout the letters of Paul, Jordan included more and more references to integration and segregation, and began making a direct link between the Jew and Gentile conflict of the first century and the black and white conflict of the twentieth. He seemed to be experimenting with those translations, and sometimes his desire to modernize the text did not result in a happy translation.

As Jordan evolved his translation style with regard to racial conflict, he also involved more issues of communal living and nonviolence. Overall, he made his Cotton Patch versions address the topics that concerned Koinonia Farm residents.

By the time Jordan had translated Matthew, Luke, and John 1–8, he was applying the texts in a very bold and direct manner to the problem of racism. We see his parable of the good Samaritan and other stories as they might have been lived in rural Georgia. Translations of the epistles touched on the topic of racism and took pieces of the texts into the twentieth century; translations of the gospels focused heavily on the problem of racism and brought Jesus directly into 1960s Georgia.

Perhaps the crowd's response to Jesus' words in the Sermon on the Mount is also applicable to the readers' responses to Jordan's Cotton Patch versions: "The people were simply amazed at his ideas, for he was teaching them like he knew what he was talking about. He didn't sound like their preachers."[53]

10

Epilogue

Jordan's Death

In 1968, Clarence Jordan worked on *The Cotton Patch Version of Luke and Acts*. It arrived from the printer in mid-October 1969. He had been ill for several days that autumn with flu-like symptoms. On October 29, feeling a little better, he went out to his study room to continue working on his version of the Gospel of John. He spent the afternoon working on chapter 8. The night before, although feeling unwell, he had participated in a spontaneous party, spurred by the arrival of some high school students. The gathering was like a hundred others that had happened at Koinonia. Jordan made popcorn and brought out some of his homemade muscadine wine, and Koinonia residents remember it as a very special evening.

Someone had gone for fruitcake from the candy kitchen. And Clarence had broken out some of the '68 wine and had teased Florence as if she had not wanted any, when in fact she had breathed the suggestion into his ear. Someone had laughingly mentioned communion, and Clarence had responded thoughtfully that the substance of communion was present.[1]

He felt better the next morning and continued with his regular schedule.

Lena Hofer, a young Hutterite woman who had recently moved to Koinonia, hoped to get Clarence's advice concerning a letter from home. In the late afternoon, Lena went to his study, and he welcomed her. She rushed through her story, worried that she was keeping him from his work. After Clarence gave her a few words of advice, she leaned over and hugged him as he sat at his desk. His body jerked suddenly, and Lena knew something was wrong. She ran back to the farm and got help. As Florence arrived, the Jordans' son Lenny said, "It's too late. He's dead."[2]

Millard Fuller and Florence went into Clarence's study and confirmed that he was indeed dead. They decided to take the body back to the house, where they laid it out on a bed. Fuller called the police to register Clarence's death. The police were supposed to send someone out to make an official death pronouncement and issue a death certificate, but no one would come. The police suggested calling a funeral home and having him brought by hearse to the hospital for the death certificate. Koinonia members knew that Clarence would have been opposed to such a useless expense, but they were not sure what to do.[3] Finally Koinonia members put the body in the station wagon and Fuller drove it into town himself. Although irritated, "he drove through Americus, thinking that Clarence was being treated in death as he had been in life, and how appropriate that was."[4]

After the body was taken to the hospital, the medical examiner and coroner did an autopsy with Florence's permission. Clarence had died of heart failure combined with pneumonia. The coroner finished the autopsy and released the body back to Koinonia members wrapped only in a sheet. Linda Fuller was given a paper sack with

Clarence's possessions, which included his clothing, some small change, and a few matches. She remembers thinking, "How appropriate for such a godly man, one who concerned himself with spiritual truths than with material possessions."[5]

Fuller arrived back at Koinonia Farm about midnight with the body, and by then a group of Koinonia residents and a few neighbors had assembled to dig a grave. Because of the warm temperatures, the residents knew Clarence would have to be buried about a day after his death.[6] Linda went into town the next morning to get the death certificate so there would be no question about the legality of the burial. The entire community thought it fitting that Jordan had died in very little pain, sitting in his little shack-like study where he had worked on his beloved Cotton Patch translations.

The Funeral

On a sloping pasture, called Picnic Hill by Koinonia residents, a handful of men worked overnight digging the grave. About 3:30 on the afternoon after Clarence had died, the Jordan family assembled and Clarence's body was put in a box which was then laid in the back of an old green van. The body was buried not in a casket, but in a plain wooden box used to ship caskets, and Clarence was dressed in his everyday work clothes. When the family arrived at the graveside, about 150 people stood nearby. Dallas Lee described the scene:

> There were a few affluent faces in the crowd, but mostly there were the dusty, callused bodies and soft spirits of those known as common folk. A few were in suits, Sunday hats, and high heels; others were barefoot and in working clothes.[7]

A much larger crowd might have assembled if there had been time to notify people around the country. People from the Hutterite communities and many former Koinonia members would surely have come. However, Jordan had not invited attention, and it seems that he would have been pleased by the simple surroundings.

Millard Fuller was asked to read from the Bible for the funeral, so he asked Florence for suggestions. Millard recalls, "She smiled and replied, 'Read any of it, Millard. He loved it all.' "[8] Fuller wrote that he chose to read from the Cotton Patch versions of 1 Peter and 1 John, because they "summarized the basics of the philosophy and religion of Clarence's life."[9] He finished with:

> Every human being is like a blade of grass,
> And his appearance is like a blossom.
> The grass dries up, the blossom falls off;
> But the Word of the Lord lives on and on.[10]

The feelings expressed at the funeral were both sadness and joy: sadness that Clarence would no longer be with them, but a deep conviction and joy in the resurrection.

A number of people at the funeral remarked on an unusual event. Millard Fuller's daughter Faith, who was two, heard people talking and singing in this way that expressed joy as well as sorrow, and she made her own contribution. As the men were shoveling the dirt onto the makeshift coffin, Faith stepped forward and sang, "Happy birthday to you, happy birthday to you, happy birthday dear Clarence, happy birthday to you."[11] Clarence Jordan was fifty-seven when he died.

Koinonia Farm Continues

Perhaps one would expect Koinonia Farm to disband after Jordan's death, especially since none of his children had stayed to carry on his legacy. However, Florence Jordan continued as a leading figure well into her seventies, lecturing on occasion, and providing stability for the community until her death in 1987. Many people have visited Koinonia Farm, now called Koinonia Partners, in recent years, and some have stayed to continue with Clarence's vision. The farm still produces pecans and peanuts, which are mainly sold through catalogues at Christmas. The orchards which he and Martin England planted continue to thrive.

Residents no longer practice what Le Roy Day calls "a total community of good," a decision made in the early 1990s.[12] Through a slow process of change, Koinonia members began to own more and more personal items. In addition, some Koinonia residents earn an income outside the farm, and it became more difficult to keep a common bank account. Koinonia Partners is more of a business and a site for ministry and less of an intense community than it had been during Clarence Jordan's lifetime. However, the people who work there still take lunch together, and a spirit of cooperation and racial reconciliation pervades the farm complex. In addition to the farming, a number of ministries are located at the farm including a daycare center and an after-school program.

The Sermon on the Mount

As in Jordan's day, the teachings of Jesus and in particular the Sermon on the Mount remain central. Volunteers and visitors are welcome from any religious faith, but actual members or those seeking membership must make a definite commitment to the Christian faith. Various groups meet for prayer during the week, and the communal noon meal includes prayer and devotional reading.[13] It appears that, contrary to many communal societies which lose their religious grounding after their founder dies, Koinonia Partners remains decidedly Christian.[14]

Koinonia Farm Offspring

While many people over the years have been influenced by Koinonia Farm and Jordan's vision of communal living, two communal groups grew directly out of Koinonia Farm's ministry: Jubilee Partners and New Hope House. Jubilee Partners began in 1979 in a rural area near Comer, Georgia, as a ministry to refugees. The first group of refugees was from Cuba, and in recent years they have also welcomed people from Vietnam and Bosnia.[15] Each year they assist about 150 displaced persons. Jubilee Partners provides English classes, temporary housing, legal help, and an orientation to life in the U.S. Members follow the original Koinonia model of living in separate homes, sharing some meals, and holding money and property in common.[16] The second communal group is New Hope House, which is located near one of Georgia's prisons in Griffin, Georgia. It provides a place for families to stay while visiting inmates. New Hope House is particularly interested in helping families of death row inmates and in fighting against the death penalty.[17]

In addition, Jordan and Koinonia Farm have influenced a number of other communities. Donald Pitzer, founder of the Communal Studies Association, lists two communities that he considers to have been "inspired" by Koinonia Farm. The first is Laetare Partners, begun in about 1970 in Rockford, Illinois; the second is Friendship House, begun in 1972 in Boise, Idaho.[18]

Habitat for Humanity

By far the best-known organization owing its beginning to Koinonia Farm is Habitat for Humanity. After Jordan's death, Millard Fuller stayed at Koinonia long enough to provide some stability to the community and to finish two housing subdivisions and a community park that had been begun by Koinonia Partners. The houses were built to provide housing for poor residents of Sumter County and also for Koinonia members. Two areas of Koinonia Farm were developed into residential areas, called Koinonia Village and Forest Park.[19]

Millard Fuller remarked, "By mid-1972, this work and other phases of Koinonia's various ministries were running smoothly . . . and I was restless to do something else."[20] That something else turned out to be building houses for the poor in Zaire and then eventually back in Georgia. By 1976, Fuller was the executive director of the new housing organization, Habitat for Humanity.[21] The international headquarters of Habitat for Humanity is still located in Americus, a few miles from Koinonia Partners.

Habitat for Humanity has grown into a worldwide organization that helps people with housing. The materials are often donated or bought at cost, and the labor is volunteered except for those jobs needing special expertise, such as the electrical work. Needy families are able to buy the homes on a non-profit, no-interest basis.

People who are to receive Habitat homes are expected to contribute sweat equity—meaning that they work on their own homes—and many recipients go on to assist with other Habitat homes.[22] While Habitat does not actively promote communal living and some of the other ideals held by Jordan, the organization has been able to implement part of his vision for helping the poor with housing, and in a much larger way than he could have dreamed.

The Cotton Patch Gospel Musical

One way that Jordan's vision of the kingdom of God has continued to flourish is through the musical *Cotton Patch Gospel*.[23] The musical score was written by Harry

Chapin in a bluegrass style to complement the Cotton Patch theme. One scriptwriter, Tom Key, is the main actor in the videotaped production, which was filmed in 1988, about six years after it was written. Cotton Patch Gospel is still performed by church groups and school drama societies. As the title implies, its script is based on Jordan's Cotton Patch versions of the Gospels. The musical is both joyful and poignant, and, although it was written thirteen years after Jordan's death, it has captured the Cotton Patch versions very well.

The Future of Koinonia Partners

In her book *Commitment and Community*, Rosabeth Moss Kanter provides a helpful analysis of communal groups in general and of Koinonia Farm in particular.[24] According to Kanter, Koinonia Partners has apparently, so far, proven that it is a successful community, avoiding the pitfalls of most utopian groups. Many communities disband within a few years of the founder's death, or they become completely focused on economic interests, to the exclusion of spiritual interests.[25] Koinonia Partners has continued for 30 years since Jordan's death—a long time in communal years, according to Kanter. Koinonia Partners is a farming business, but it has not lost its spiritual center.

Kanter has a list of successful and unsuccessful communal groups, based on her own criteria, but does not list Koinonia Farm in either.[26] She does, however, use Koinonia as an example of a 'service commune' that has lasted more than twenty-five years, in contrast to other communities:[27]

Critics argue that communes do not last over long periods of time, with most of them failing after only a short time, or that if they do survive, they immediately lose their vitality, institutionalizing static routines that become even less meaningful to later generations than they were to the first.[28]

Koinonia Farm/Partners has not fallen prey to either of those problems. It has lasted more than fifty-five years and does not appear to be losing its energy or vision. It has not lost its vitality or become static; rather, Koinonia Partners continues to change and grow as the surrounding area has needs. Many communal groups seem to be stuck in an era long past, but Partners is growing as their surroundings grow.

It does not look like a 1940s farm cooperative or a 1960s hippie commune. It is a twenty-first century farm business and ministry center that is keeping up with the times. In addition, Koinonia Partners has not lost its religious basis, even though the founder has died and current residents were not there to help draft the original vision. Communal groups do not last indefinitely, but Koinonia Partners seems to be going strong and will probably continue well into the future.

❋   ❋   ❋

Clarence Jordan wanted Koinonia Farm to be a demonstration plot for the kingdom of God. He used passages from the New Testament, mainly the Sermon on the Mount and Acts 2 and 4, to develop the three touchstones of Koinonia: pacifism, racial reconciliation, and communal living. At different points in the history of the farm, those three elements had different emphases, but the underlying belief system remained.

Jordan was trying to live out the kingdom of God as he saw it in the New Testament and as he thought it would translate into twentieth century rural Georgia. His ideas regarding the kingdom in modern times can be seen in his Cotton Patch versions of the New Testament books. After his death, Koinonia Partners has continued to follow his vision, while making some changes in its concept of communal living.

Jordan's early life prepared him to wrestle with issues of theology as well as race relations. Raised in a Southern Baptist household, he became familiar with the importance of God's love through sermons, songs, and the Bible. However, he began also to see the evils of racism in rural Georgia, often in the same people who were preaching and singing about God's love. Among others, his experience of living near a jail and getting to know some of the prisoners contributed to his desire to fight racism and cruelty.

His college years at the University of Georgia added more to his vision of the Christian life through his intense personal study of the Sermon on the Mount. His resulting adoption of a pacifist stance was quite unusual in a southern Baptist gentleman. Studies in the field of agriculture also provided him with information about farming that he later used to begin his community. Jordan's early idea was to live out his Christian beliefs by helping African-American sharecroppers get ahead financially, using the newer farm techniques he had learned at college. However, by the end of his college years, he was moved also by a desire to learn more about the Christian faith and to preach.

Jordan developed a deep and long-lasting interest in biblical Greek during his years at Southern Baptist Theological Seminary. In studying the New Testament, he was struck by the kind of community he saw among the early Christian believers. He loved word studies, and his understanding of *koinonia* brought communal living into his vision for the Christian life. He also identified the importance of the kingdom of God, particularly as it is presented in Matthew's Gospel.

Meanwhile, Jordan was given opportunities to teach African-American students in Louisville, and his anger against racism was rekindled. By the time he finished seminary, the idea of living out the kingdom of God in a radical way had gripped him. Along with Martin England, he developed the three ideas of racial reconciliation, pacifism, and communal living as the foundation for a new way of living the Christian life.

The early years of Koinonia Farm were spent struggling to get the operation up and running. However, Jordan and England remained committed to their interpretation of the Christian faith, even when it led to difficult relationships in the community. Jordan was able to begin some ministries such as vacation Bible school and farm technique lectures, and people began to come to Koinonia Farm, some to visit and some to stay. The Jordans and other Koinonia Farm families became involved with the local Southern Baptist church. Although the situation was much more difficult than he had imagined, Koinonia Farm families began to live out Jordan's vision for the kingdom of God.

By the 1950s, the steady persecution of Koinonia Farm made life very hard for Koinonia members. There was a sense of standing for a right cause in the face of persecution, but there was also fear. The persecution, which resulted in a break with the Southern Baptist church, did not keep Koinonia members from their work. They continued to find comfort in accounts of the persecution of the early Christians.

Through his preaching around the country and his book *Sermon on the Mount,* Jordan's ideas became better known. *Sermon on the Mount* was important because it showed his focus on the kingdom of God. He was not primarily fighting racism. He was not primarily arguing for nonviolent approaches to anger. He was not primarily beginning a commune. Rather, Jordan was primarily a student of Scripture who wanted to live out his understanding of the biblical lifestyle. His choice of subject for his first book and his decision to preach around the country instead of lecturing on those secondary topics further point to his theologically driven views.

The unsettled years of the 1960s contributed to the confusion about Jordan's intentions. Many visitors to Koinonia Farm came because they were interested solely in the civil rights movement, in full swing. Anti-war demonstrators came because they admired Jordan's pacifist stand. Hippies came because they rejected American materialism and were interested in communal living. A large number of those people, many of them college students, were disappointed and confused by the Christian emphasis at Koinonia.

The confusion of those guests highlights Jordan's emphasis on the theological foundations of Koinonia Farm. When Millard Fuller arrived and helped reorganize Koinonia Farm into Koinonia Partners, the underlying motivation continued to be the desire to live out the kingdom, but in new ways.

The Cotton Patch versions also reveal Jordan's theological vision. He chose to write updated versions of the Scriptures, and his choice of texts is quite significant. He might have spent his time writing more generally about racial reconciliation, pacifism, and communal living, perhaps including religion as a fourth topic. Certainly that would have fit with many authors' descriptions of Koinonia Farm's purpose. Religion might have been one of a handful of important topics. Jordan, however, chose to reinterpret the New Testament. In those new versions, his views on race, pacifism, and community (which he would have argued were *not* his ideas, but rather were found in the original texts) unfolded.

After Jordan's death, the community sought to carry on by working to make the vision of Koinonia Partners a reality. Millard Fuller, pursuing the ideas that he had discussed with Jordan, began Habitat for Humanity. Habitat reflects Fuller's personality more than Jordan's, but the main vision for the organization came from Jordan and his desire to demonstrate God's kingdom.

Koinonia Partners, too, has changed over the years. Some of those changes would probably please Jordan, such as the fact that Koinonia Partners is now much more interracial than Koinonia Farm was able to be in the 1940s, 1950s, and 1960s. Some of the changes would probably dishearten him, such as the decision to no longer hold communal finances. However, in general, Koinonia Partners continues as a testimony to Jordan's vision; it is a demonstration plot for the kingdom of God. It remains to be seen how long Jordan's vision will last at Koinonia Partners, but certainly the theology that Jordan put forth has had a lasting influence on thousands of people through his writings, his recorded sermons, visits to Koinonia over the years, and Habitat for Humanity.

Notes

Chapter 1

1. Henlee H. Barnette, *Clarence Jordan: Turning Dreams into Deeds* (Macon Ga.: Smyth & Helwys Publishing, 1992), 6.

2. Walter Bauer, *A Greek-English Lexicon of the New Testament and Other Early Christian Literature,* 2d ed., trans. and adapted by William F. Arndt and F. Wilbur Gingrich; rev. and augmented by F. Wilbur Gingrich and Frederick W. Danker (Chicago: University of Chicago Press, 1979), 438-9.

3. *A Look at Koinonia* (Americus, Ga.: Koinonia Partners, 1997), 2.

4. For example, see Jordan's sermon entitled *"Incarnational Evangelism"* in *The Substance of Faith and Other Cotton Patch Sermons* by Clarence Jordan, ed. Dallas Lee (New York: Association Press, 1972), 31-7.

5. Tracy Elaine K'Meyer, *Interracialism and Christian Community in the Postwar South: The Story of Koinonia Farm* (Charlottesville, Va.: University Press of Virginia, 1997).

6. K'Meyer in *Interracialism and Christian Community* includes very few of these stories. Most of the stories come from Jordan's sermons or from Dallas Lee's book *The Cotton Patch Evidence: The Story of Clarence Jordan and the Koinonia Farm Experiment (1942-1970)* (New York: Harper & Row, 1971).

7. Matthew 5–7.

8. Clarence Jordan, *Sermon on the Mount* (Valley Forge, Pa.: Judson Press, 1952).

Chapter 2

1. Katherine L. Dvorak, *An African-American Exodus: The Segregation of the Southern Churches* (Brooklyn, N.Y.: Carlson Publishing, 1991), 169; also, Paul Harvey, *Redeeming the South: Religious Cultures and Racial Identities Among Southern Baptists 1865-1925* (Chapel Hill, N.C.: The University of North Carolina Press, 1997), 12.

2. Dvorak, 169.

3. Harvey, 12.

4. Ibid.

5. Nathan O. Hatch, *The Democratization of American Christianity* (New Haven, Conn.: Yale University Press, 1989).

6. Tracy Elaine K'Meyer, *Interracialism and Christian Community in the Postwar South: The Story of Koinonia Farm* (Charlottesville, Va.: University Press of Virginia, 1997), 257.

7. P. Joel Snider, *The "Cotton Patch" Gospel: The Proclamation of Clarence Jordan* (New York: University of America Press, 1985), 8. See also K'Meyer, 26.

8. K'Meyer, *Interracialism*, 257.

9. Clarence Jordan, "The Meaning of *Thanatos and Nekros* in the Epistles of Paul," unpublished doctoral dissertation, Southern Baptist Theological Seminary, Louisville, Ky., 1938; also see Snider, *The "Cotton Patch" Gospel*, 7.

10. Clarence Jordan Papers, Hargrett Rare Book and Manuscript Library, University of Georgia Libraries, Athens, Ga., Manuscript #756, Boxes 1 and 2; also, Snider, *The "Cotton Patch" Gospel, 8.*

11. Clarence Jordan Papers, #756, Box 1, Folder 7.

12. Snider, *The "Cotton Patch" Gospel*, 8.

13. K'Meyer, *Interracialism*, 26.

14. Dallas Lee, *The Cotton Patch Evidence: The Story of Clarence Jordan and the Koinonia Farm Experiment (1942-1970)* (New York: Harper & Row, 1971), 7.

15. Ibid., 6.

16. Snider, *The "Cotton Patch" Gospel*, 8; also see Lee, *The Cotton Patch Evidence*, 6.

17. Koinonia Partners tape collection, #CJ58D, Interview with Frank, George, and Lillian Jordan, n.d.

18. K'Meyer, *Interracialism*, 26.

19. See grade reports in Clarence Jordan Papers, #756, Box 9, Folder 2.

20. Clarence Jordan Papers, #756 Box 1, Folder 1, February 4, 1927, letter from Buddie to Jordan. Buddie was in college, and Jordan was a sophomore at Talbotton High School.

21. Koinonia Partners tape collection, #CJ58D, Interview with Frank, George, and Lillian Jordan, n.d.

22. K'Meyer, *Interracialism*, 26.

23. Lee, *Cotton Patch Evidence*, 7-8.

24. Ibid., 8.

25. K'Meyer, *Interracialism*, 27.

26. Lee, *Cotton Patch Evidence*, 8-9; Koinonia Partners tape collection, #CJ56, "Clarence Jordan Tells the Koinonia Story," n.d.; K'Meyer, *Interracialism*, 27.

27. Lee, *Cotton Patch Evidence*, 9.

28. Ibid., 9-10.

29. Ibid., 10.

30. Snider, *The "Cotton Patch" Gospel*, 9.

31. Clarence Jordan Papers, #756, Box 1, Folder 3, Talbotton High School Graduation Program, June 3, 1929.

32. Lee, *Cotton Patch Evidence*, 10.

33. James McClendon, *Biography as Theology: How Life Stories Can Remake Today's Theology* (Nashville, Tenn.: Abingdon Press, 1974), 92.

34. K'Meyer, *Interracialism*, 27-8.

35. Clarence Jordan Papers, #756, Box 1, Folder 4, March 17, 1930, letter from Clarence Jordan to his mother.

36. K'Meyer, *Interracialism*, 28.

37. Clarence Jordan Papers, #756, Box 1, Folder 3, September 16, 1929, letter from Clarence Jordan to his mother.

38. Clarence Jordan Papers, #756, Box 1, Folder 6, Spring 1932, Jordan wrote letters on Baptist Student Union stationery with his name and the title of president printed in the upper left corner.

39. K'Meyer, *Interracialism*, 28.

40. Lee, *Cotton Patch Evidence*, 12.

41. McClendon, *Biography as Theology*, 92.

42. Lee, *Cotton Patch Evidence*, 13; Snider, *The "Cotton Patch" Gospel*, 10.

43. Snider, 10.

44. Lee, *Cotton Patch Evidence*, 14.

45. McClendon, *Biography as Theology*, 92.

46. Clarence Jordan Papers, #756, Box 1, Folder 7, n.d. For example, Jordan preached as a guest at the East Athens Baptist Church.

47. Lee, *Cotton Patch Evidence*, 11.

48. Clarence Jordan Papers, #756, Box 1, Folder 7; Lee, *Cotton Patch Evidence*, 14.

49. Lee, 15.

Chapter 3

1. James McClendon, *Biography as Theology: How Life Stories Can Remake Today's Theology* (Nashville, Tenn.: Abingdon Press, 1974), 93.

2. Dallas Lee, *The Cotton Patch Evidence: The Story of Clarence Jordan and the Koinonia Farm Experiment (1942-1970)* (New York: Harper & Row. 1971), 15.

3. P. Joel Snider, *The "Cotton Patch" Gospel: The Proclamation Of Clarence Jordan* (New York: University of America Press, 1985), 11.

4. Ibid.; *Jordan's italics.*

5. *Clarence Jordan, "The Distinct Identity," in The Substance of Faith and Other Cotton Patch Sermons by Clarence Jordan,* ed. Dallas Lee (New York: Association Press, 1972), 108.

6. McClendon, *Biography as Theology,* 93.

7. Henlee H. Barnette, *Clarence Jordan: Turning Dreams into Deeds* (Macon, Ga.: Smyth & Helwys Publishing, 1992), 14.

8. Ibid.

9. Ibid., 13-4.

10. One might expect Greek scholar A. T. Robertson to have influenced Jordan, and certainly he had impacted the seminary in general, but he was ill and died while Jordan was a student.

11. Tracy Elaine K'Meyer, *Interracialism and Christian Community in the Postwar South: The Story of Koinonia Farm* (Charlottesville, Va.: University Press of Virginia, 1997), 29. Although Jordan never discussed Karl Barth or espoused his theology directly, he may have been somewhat influenced by Barth's theology of the Word through McDowell.

12. Clarence Jordan Papers, Hargrett Rare Book and Manuscript Library, University of Georgia Libraries, Athens, Ga., Manuscript #756, Box 6, Folder 9, letter from Clarence Jordan to Edward A. McDowell Jr., May 29, 1964.

13. Snider, *The "Cotton Patch" Gospel,* 11.

14. Ibid.

15. Clarence Jordan Papers, #756, Box 1, Folder 9.

16. Lee, *Cotton Patch Evidence,* 16; McClendon, *Biography as Theology,* 94.

17. Snider, *The "Cotton Patch" Gospel,* 11.

18. McClendon, *Biography as Theology,* 94.

19. Lee, *Cotton Patch Evidence,* 17.

20. Ibid.

21. Ibid.

22. Snider, *The "Cotton Patch" Gospel,* 11.

23. Clarence Jordan Papers, #756, Box 1, Folder 10, letter to Clarence Jordan from his father, May 19, 1936.

24. Koinonia Partners tape CJ56, "Clarence Jordan Tells the Koinonia Story," n.d.

25. Clarence Jordan Papers #756, Box 1, Folder 8; letter from Clarence Jordan to his mother, October 1934.

26. K'Meyer, *Interracialism*, 32.

27. Ibid.

28. Lee, *Cotton Patch Evidence*, 20; see also K'Meyer, *Interracialism*, 32.

29. Lee, *Cotton Patch Evidence*, 20.

30. Ibid., 21.

31. Ibid.

32. Snider, *The "Cotton Patch" Gospel*, 12.

33. K'Meyer, *Interracialism*, 32-3.

34. Lee, *Cotton Patch Evidence*, 21.

35. McClendon, *Biography as Theology*, 94.

36. Clarence Jordan Papers, #756, Box 1, Folder 11, letters from Clarence to local churches, March 1939 and November 15, 1939.

37. K'Meyer, *Interracialism*, 32-3.

38. Ibid., 33.

39. Snider, *The "Cotton Patch" Gospel*, 12.

40. Clarence Jordan Papers #756, Box 1, Folder 11, letter from the Kentucky Baptist Woman's Missionary Union to the Long Run Association, January 23, 1939.

41. Lee, *Cotton Patch Evidence*, 22.

42. Ibid., 22-3.

43. Ibid., 23-4.

44. K'Meyer, *Interracialism*, 33.

45. Clarence Jordan Papers, #756, Box 15, Folder 2, Long Run Association Program, 1942.

46. Clarence Jordan Papers, #756, Box 24, Folder 4, News Release, March 15, 1940.

47. Acts 2:44-45 and 4:32, King James Version (one of the English versions Jordan used), *my emphases*.

48. Walter Bauer, *A Greek-English Lexicon of the New Testament and Other Early Christian Literature*, 2d ed., trans. and adapted by William F. Arndt and F. Wilbur Gingrich; rev. and augmented by F. Wilbur Gingrich and Frederick W. Danker (Chicago: University of Chicago Press, 1979), 438.

49. Barnette, *Clarence Jordan: Turning Dreams into Deeds*, 17.

50. Lee, *Cotton Patch Evidence*, 25.

51. Barnette, *Clarence Jordan: Turning Dreams into Deeds,* 17-9; K'Meyer, *Interracialism,* 31; Lee, *Cotton Patch Evidence,* 26.

52. Clarence Jordan Papers, #756, Box 2, Folder 2, letter from William Hall Preston to Clarence Jordan, March 4, 1942, unusual use of the third person.

53. K'Meyer, *Interracialism,* 35.

54. For example, see "Racial Frontiers," *Baptist Student.* (November, 1941): 6-7.

55. Tracy Elaine K'Meyer, *Koinonia Farm: Building the Beloved Community in Postwar Georgia,* dissertation (Ann Arbor, Mich.: UMI Press, 1993), 31.

56. Martin Luther King Jr. also graduated from Crozer. Prof. "Snuffy" Smith's ethics classes impacted King and perhaps impacted England. Crozer Seminary merged with Colgate Rochester Divinity School in 1970.

57. K'Meyer, *Interracialism,* 35-6.

58. Lee, *Cotton Patch Evidence,* 29.

59. Ibid., 27-8.

60. Snider, *The "Cotton Patch" Gospel,* 13.

61. K'Meyer, *Interracialism,* 36; Lee, *Cotton Patch Evidence,* 29.

62. Lee, *Cotton Patch Evidence,* 29.

Chapter 4

1. Clarence Jordan Papers, Hargrett Rare Book and Manuscript Library, University of Georgia Libraries, Athens, Ga., Manuscript #2341, Box 3, Folder 8, Letter from Martin England to Henlee Barnette, n.d.; Tracy Elaine K'Meyer, *Interracialism and Christian Community in the Postwar South: The Story of Koinonia Farm* (Charlottesville, Va.: University Press of Virginia, 1997), 36.

2. Clarence Jordan Papers, #756, Box 15, Folder 1, letter from Martin England to Dr. Howard, May 17, 1942, 36.

3. K'Meyer, *Interracialism,* 36.

4. Clarence Jordan, "Dr. Jordan's Statement," *The Longrunner,* (August 1942): 2.

5. Lee, *Cotton Patch Evidence,* 30.

6. K'Meyer, *Interracialism,* 41.

7. Lee, *Cotton Patch Evidence,* 30-1.

8. Ibid., 31.

9. Ibid.

10. K'Meyer, *Interracialism,* 39-40.

11. Ibid., 38-9.

12. Lee, *Cotton Patch Evidence*, 32.

13. K'Meyer, *Interracialism*, 38.

14. Ibid., 39.

15. Lee, *Cotton Patch Evidence*, 33.

16. Ibid.

17. Ibid.

18. Ibid., 31; Clarence Jordan Papers, #756, Box 2, Folder 2, letters from Marjorie Moore to Clarence Jordan, May 16, 1942, and May 21, 1942; Howard G. McClain in *Koinonia Remembered: The First Fifty Years,* Kay N. Weiner, ed. (Americus, Ga.: Koinonia Partners, 1992), 4.

19. Lee, *Cotton Patch Evidence*, 31-2.

20. Ibid., 32.

21. Ibid.

22. Ibid., 33-4.

23. Clarence Jordan Papers, #2340, Box 1, letter from Martin England to Mack Goss, July 15, 1942.

24. Clarence Jordan Papers, #756, Box 26, Folder 5, Sumter County Farm Statistics.

25. K'Meyer, *Interracialism,* 40.

26. P. Joel Snider, *The "Cotton Patch" Gospel: The Proclamation of Clarence Jordan* (New York: University Press of America, 1985), 14.

27. Lee, *The Cotton Patch Evidence*, 35.

28. Tracy Elaine K'Meyer, *Koinonia Farm: Building the Beloved Community in Postwar Georgia,* dissertation (Ann Arbor, Mich.: UMI Press, 1993), 42.

29. Lee, *Cotton Patch Evidence*, 35.

30. Beverly England Williams in *Koinonia Remembered,* ed. Weiner, 11.

31. Ibid.

32. K'Meyer, *Interracialism,* 43; Lee, *Cotton Patch Evidence,* 36, 41.

33. Lee, *Cotton Patch Evidence*, 41.

34. Acts 2:44-45 and 4:32.

35. K'Meyer, *Interracialism,* 43.

36. Ibid.

37. Snider, 15.

38. Ibid.

39. K'Meyer, *Interracialism,* 43.

Chapter 5

1. Dallas Lee, *The Cotton Patch Evidence: The Story of Clarence Jordan and the Koinonia Farm Experiment (1942-1970)* (New York: Harper & Row, 1971), 36.

2. Clarence Jordan Papers, Hargrett Rare Book and Manuscript Library, University of Georgia Libraries, Athens, Ga., Manuscript #756, Box 2, Folder 3, letter from Koinonia Farm to ministry partners, December 1942; P. Joel Snider, *The "Cotton Patch" Gospel: The Proclamation of Clarence Jordan* (New York: University of America Press, 1985), 14.

3. Tracy Elaine K'Meyer, *Koinonia Farm: Building the Beloved Community in Postwar Georgia,* dissertation (Ann Arbor, Mich.: UMI Press, 1993), 43.

4. Lee, *Cotton Patch Evidence*, 36.

5. Snider, *The "Cotton Patch" Gospel*, 14.

6. Lee, *Cotton Patch Evidence*, 41.

7. Ibid., 40-1.

8. "The Fighting South: It Knows that War Is Hell But that Hell Is Better than Dishonor," *Life* 13:1 (6 July 1942): 57-71. See also Lee, *Cotton Patch Evidence*, 2-3.

9. "Fighting South," 57.

10. Clarence Jordan, *The Substance of Faith and Other Cotton Patch Sermons by Clarence Jordan*, ed. Dallas Lee (New York: Association Press, 1972), 7.

11. Lee, *Cotton Patch Evidence*, 54.

12. Ibid., 58; also Clarence Jordan, "The Christian, War, Violence, and Nonviolence," in Henlee H. Barnette, *Clarence Jordan: Turning Dreams into Deeds* (Macon, Ga.: Smyth & Helwys Publishing, 1992), 27-8.

13. Tracy Elaine K'Meyer, *Interracialism and Christian Community in the Postwar South: The Story of Koinonia Farm* (Charlottesville, Va.: University Press of Virginia, 1997), 57.

14. Lee, *Cotton Patch Evidence*, 37.

15. Ibid., 37-8.

16. Ibid., 38.

17. Ibid., 38-9.

18. Snider, *The "Cotton Patch" Gospel*, 15-6, see also, K'Meyer, *Interracialism*, 51.

19. Lee, *Cotton Patch Evidence*, 42.

20. Ibid.

21. Snider, *The "Cotton Patch" Gospel,* 16; Lee, *Cotton Patch Evidence,* 42-3.

22. Lee, 43.

23. K'Meyer, *Interracialism,* 83-4.

24. Lee, *Cotton Patch Evidence,* 39.

25. Ibid., 40.

26. Ibid.

27. Snider, *The "Cotton Patch" Gospel,* 15.

28. Clarence Jordan Papers, Box 2, letter from D. B. Nicholson to J. W. Jordan, July 31, 1944.

29. Snider, *The "Cotton Patch" Gospel,* 15.

30. For a list of regular Koinonia residents during the 1940s, see K'Meyer, *Interracialism,* 65.

31. Ibid., 44-5.

32. Lee, *Cotton Patch Evidence,* 45-6.

33. Ibid., 46.

34. Ibid.

35. Ibid.

36. Ibid., 46-7. Atkinson was exempt from the draft because he was about to enter seminary. He was given a ministerial exemption.

37. Ibid., 47.

38. Ibid., 48-9.

39. Harry Atkinson in *Koinonia Remembered: The First Fifty Years,*. Kay N. Weiner, ed. (Americus, Ga.: Koinonia Partners, 1992), 19.

40. Lee, *Cotton Patch Evidence,* 49.

41. Ibid., 47.

42. K'Meyer, *Koinonia Farm,* 72.

43. Lee, *Cotton Patch Evidence,* 84.

44. Ibid., 47.

45. Ibid.

46. K'Meyer, *Interracialism,* 67.

47. Ibid., 65.

48. Ibid., 71; Lee, *Cotton Patch Evidence,* 43.

49. Lee, 44-5.

50. Snider, *The "Cotton Patch" Gospel,* 16.

51. Ibid., 16-7.

52. Sara M. Owen in *Koinonia Remembered,* Weiner, ed., 25.

53. G. McLeod Bryan in *Koinonia Remembered,* Weiner, ed., 13-4.

54. Lee, *Cotton Patch Evidence,* 45.

55. Ibid.

56. Marjorie M. Armstrong in *Koinonia Remembered*, Weiner, ed., 8-9.

57. K'Meyer, *Koinonia Farm*, 45.

58. Lee, *Cotton Patch Evidence*, 43.

59. Ibid., 43-4.

60. "Koinonia Farm: Second Anniversary," Koinonia Partners Archives, Americus, Ga., 1944.

61. K'Meyer, *Interracialism*, 46.

62. Lee, *Cotton Patch Evidence*, 43.

63. Snider, *The "Cotton Patch" Gospel*, 16.

64. Lee, *Cotton Patch Evidence*, 44.

65. K'Meyer, *Interracialism*, 47.

66. Ibid.

Chapter 6

1. Dallas Lee, *The Cotton Patch Evidence: The Story of Clarence Jordan and the Koinonia Farm Experiment (1942-1970)* (New York: Harper & Row, 1971), 74-5.

2. Ibid., 75.

3. P. Joel Snider, *The "Cotton Patch" Gospel: The Proclamation of Clarence Jordan* (New York: University of America Press, 1985), 17.

4. Lee, *Cotton Patch Evidence*, 75.

5. Ibid., 76.

6. Clarence Jordan Papers, Hargrett Rare Book and Manuscript Library, University of Georgia Libraries, Athens, Ga., Manuscript #756, Box 2, Folder 13, letter from Ira B. Flaglier to Clarence Jordan, August 9, 1950.

7. Lee, *Cotton Patch Evidence*, 76-7.

8. The full text can be found in Lee, *Cotton Patch Evidence*, 77-8, and is as follows:

Whereas, Mr. & Mrs. C. L. Jordan, Miss Eleanor Jordan, Mr. & Mrs. Howard Johnson, and Miss Willie Pugh, members of Rehoboth Baptist Church, are also members of Koinonia Farm, an organization actively engaged in advocating views and practices contrary to those of other members of the Rehoboth Church, and

Whereas, representatives of this group have brought people of other races into the services of the Rehoboth Baptist Church, and have done this with the knowledge that such practices were not in accord with the practices of other members of Rehoboth Church, and

Whereas, said members do constantly visit Negro churches in the community, and have persisted in holding services where both white and colored attend together, and

Whereas, said members, because of these views and practices, have caused serious friction in our church, and have disrupted the Christian unity and spirit which had previously prevailed, and

Whereas, some members of Koinonia Farm have misbehaved, and created disturbances in our services, more than once, attempting to draw the attention of others, and

Whereas, the leaders of Koinonia Farm have made remarks that seemed unchristian, and have stated that they do not agree with certain doctrines and policies of the Baptist church, and they admit that they do not know what their relationship to the local church should be, and

Whereas, said leaders have stated that they are trying to convert individuals to their ideas and would like to see members added to their own group, we do not feel they are working for the best interest of the Rehoboth Church, and

Whereas, members of Koinonia Farm have stated that the church is possibly operated under false doctrines (not holding the truth), and that it might be best for the present organization to collapse, and

Whereas, after much prayer and consideration, and after consulting many pastors and laymen of other Baptist churches, we feel that said members are no longer in full fellowship of our church, and that it will be to the best interest of the spiritual welfare and progress of our church to withdraw fellowship from them.

Therefore, we recommend that the Rehoboth Baptist Church do on this 13th day of August, 1950, withdraw fellowship from any who are members of Koinonia Farm, and that their names be stricken from the church roll.

9. Ibid., 79.

10. Snider, *The "Cotton Patch" Gospel*, 18.

11. Ibid.

12. Lee, *Cotton Patch Evidence*, 79.

13. Ibid., 80.

14. Ibid.

15. Ibid., 80-1.

16. Ibid., 81.

17. Ibid.

18. Rosabeth Moss Kanter, *Commitment and Community: Communes and Utopias in Sociological Perspective* (Cambridge: Harvard University, 1972), 61-161.

19. Tracy Elaine K'Meyer, *Interracialism and Christian Community in the Postwar South: The Story of Koinonia Farm* (Charlottesville, Va.: University Press of Virginia, 1997), 69-70.

20. Lee, *Cotton Patch Evidence*, 82.

21. This is opposite of the usual order of events in communal groups as observed by Kanter, 157-61. Most communal groups begin with a utopian vision of community that develops later into an economic system, often only becoming an economic system when the community is moving toward dissolution.

22. Lee, *Cotton Patch Evidence*, 82-3.

23. Ibid., 82; Clarence Jordan Papers, #756, Box 3, Folder 1, notes from Koinonia meeting, October 2, 1954, show that this conflict persisted.

24. Lee, *Cotton Patch Evidence*, 82.

25. Ibid., 82-3.

26. Ibid., 83.

27. Ibid.

28. Clarence Jordan Papers, #2341, Box 4, Folder 11, original signed statement of commitment, written and first signed April 21, 1951, and last signed December 29, 1959.

29. Clarence Jordan Papers, #2341, Box 4, Folder 11, original signed statement of commitment. There are two dates next to Ross Anderson's name, December 29, 1959 and November 1958.

30. Lee, *Cotton Patch Evidence*, 84.

31. Ibid., 86.

32. Ibid.

33. Ibid., 87.

34. Ibid.

35. Snider, *The "Cotton Patch" Gospel*, 19.

36. Lee, *Cotton Patch Evidence*, 106.

37. Ibid.

38. K'Meyer, *Interracialism*, 89.

39. Ibid.

40. Lee, *Cotton Patch Evidence*, 107.

41. K'Meyer, *Interracialism*, 89.

42. Lee, *Cotton Patch Evidence*, 107.

43. Ibid., 108.

44. K'Meyer, *Interracialism*, 89.

45. Ibid., 85.

46. Ibid.

47. Ibid., 85-6.

48. Lee, *Cotton Patch Evidence*, 109.

49. Ibid., 110.

50. Ibid.

51. Ibid.

52. Ibid., 111.

53. Ibid., 113-4.

54. Ibid., 111.

55. Koinonia Partners tape collection, #CJ58F, interview with Con and Ora Browne, n.d.

56. Lee, *Cotton Patch Evidence*, 111.

57. Snider, *The "Cotton Patch" Gospel*, 21.

58. K'Meyer, *Interracialism*, 93.

59. Lee, *Cotton Patch Evidence*, 113.

60. Ibid., 114.

61. K'Meyer, *Interracialism*, 86.

62. Lee, *Cotton Patch Evidence*, 111-2.

63. Ibid., 112.

64. K'Meyer, *Interracialism*, 87.

65. Ibid.

66. Ibid.

67. Ibid., 87-8.

68. Lee, *Cotton Patch Evidence*, 112.

69. Ibid., 112-3.

70. "Embattled Fellowship Farm," *Time* (Sept. 17, 1956): 79-80; "Embattled Koinonia," *Time* (Apr. 29, 1957): 44-5; "Every Man's Land—Or No Man's Land," *Newsweek* (Feb. 25, 1957): 37; Andre Fontaine, "The Conflict in a Southern Town," *Redbook* (Oct. 1957): 48-50.

71. "Other Cheek Is Turned in Georgia Bombing," *The Christian Century* 73 (Aug. 22, 1956): 965; Robert Lee, "The Crisis at Koinonia," *The Christian Century* 73 (Nov. 7, 1956): 1290-1; "The Spirit of Koinonia," *The Christian Century* 74 (Feb. 13, 1957): 185; "Terrorists Attack Koinonia Farm," *The Christian Century* 74 (Feb. 13, 1957): 187; "Koinonia Farm Under Siege," *The Christian Century* 72 (Feb. 20, 1957): 219; Eugene Lipman, "Report on a Siege," *The Christian Century* (Feb. 25, 1957): 233-5; "Creative Church in Georgia," *The Christian Century* 74 (Mar. 6, 1957): 285-287; "Argument Returns to Violence," *The Christian Century* 72 (June 26, 1957): 780.

72. Lee, *Cotton Patch Evidence*, 113.

73. Ibid.

74. Clarence Jordan Papers, #756, Box 2, Folder 14, 1951.

75. John A. Hostetler, *Hutterite Society* (Baltimore: Johns Hopkins University Press, 1974), 1.

76. Ibid., 279-80.

77. Ibid., 280-2. For information on the reconciliation between the Hutterites and the Bruderhof colonies in the early 1970s and the subsequent split in the early 1990s, see Hostetler, 280-2 and J. Christoph Arnold, "An Open Letter from the Bruderhof," *Plough* 41 (Winter 1995): 2-6.

78. Clarence Jordan Papers, #756, Box 3, Folder 2, January 4, 1955.

79. Clarence Jordan Papers, Manuscript #756, Box 3, letters.

80. Clarence Jordan Papers, #756, Box 3, Folder 1, December 1954, Koinonia Christmas letter.

81. Lee, *Cotton Patch Evidence,* 166-7.

82. Ibid., 168.

83. Ibid., 168-9.

84. Ibid., 171.

85. Ibid., 169-70.

86. William D. Miller, *Dorothy Day: A Biography* (San Francisco: Harper & Row, 1982), 441.

87. William D. Miller, *A Harsh and Dreadful Love: Dorothy Day and the Catholic Worker Movement* (New York: Liveright, 1973), 253-4.

88. K'Meyer, *Interracialism,* 97.

89. Clarence Jordan Papers, #756, Box 4, March 7, 1957, letter from Clarence Jordan to Claude Broach.

Chapter 7

1. Clarence Jordan, *Sermon on the Mount* (Valley Forge, Pa.: Judson Press, 1952). The text is found in Matthew 5-7.

2. Some of Jordan's early sermons and lectures were preserved on reel-to-reel recordings, which have since been copied onto cassettes.

3. Jordan, *Sermon,* 9.

4. Dallas Lee, *The Cotton Patch Evidence, The Story of Clarence Jordan and the Koinonia Farm Experiment (1942-1970)* (New York: Harper & Row, 1971), 172.

5. Jordan, *Sermon,* 18.

6. Ibid. *Jordan's italics.*

7. Ibid., 19. See Matthew 5:5-13 and John 3:3.

8. Ibid., 20.

9. Ibid., 36-7.

10. Ibid., 63.

11. Ibid., 93, *Jordan's italics*.

12. Ibid., 126.

13. Donald E. Pitzer, ed., *America's Communal Utopias* (Chapel Hill, N.C.: University of North Carolina Press, 1997), 37-87 and 319-51; Benjamin Zablocki, *The Joyful Community* (Baltimore: Penguin Books, 1971), particularly chapter 7, "A Model for Utopia?" 286-326.

14. "Blessed are those who are persecuted for righteousness' sake, for theirs is the kingdom of heaven. Blessed are you when people revile you and persecute you and utter all kinds of evil against you falsely on my account. Rejoice and be glad, for your reward is great in heaven, for in the same way they persecuted the prophets who were before you."

15. Oliver and Cris Popenoe, *Seeds of Tomorrow* (New York: Harper & Row, 1984), 279.

16. Le Roy J. Day, "Koinonia Partners: An Intentional Community Since 1942," *Communal Societies* 10 (1990): 123. See also Popenoe, *Seeds of Tomorrow*, 279-80.

17. Day, "Koinonia Partners," 123.

18. Many of these sermons can be ordered from Koinonia Records, Route 2, Americus, Ga., 31709.

19. Clarence Jordan, *Power from Parables*, No. 3, cassette, Koinonia Records, Americus, Ga., n.d., *Jordan's emphasis*.

20. Clarence Jordan, "The Humanity of God" in *The Substance of Faith and Other Cotton Patch Sermons by Clarence Jordan*, ed. Dallas Lee (New York: Association Press, 1972), 30.

21. Jordan, "Incarnational Evangelism" in *Substance of Faith* 31. See John 1:14.

22. Jordan, "Judas" in *Substance of Faith*, 124.

23. Ibid.

24. Ibid., 125-6.

25. Ibid., 126.

26. Ibid., 127.

27. Jordan, "The Humanity of God" in *Substance of Faith*, 24.

28. Ibid., *my italics*.

29. Ibid., 26-30; *Peter* comes from the word *petros* meaning *rock* or *stone* in Greek, and Bar-Jonah can be translated son of John, therefore Johnson.

30. Jordan, "The Mind of Christ in the Racial Conflict" in *Substance of Faith*, 105, *Jordan's italics*.

31. Jordan, "The Mind of Christ in the Racial Conflict" in *Substance of Faith,* 105.

32. Ibid.

33. Jordan, "Incarnational Evangelism" in *Substance of Faith,* 3.

34. Jordan, "Was Jesus Really Poor?" in *Substance of Faith,* 86.

35. Jordan, "Incarnational Evangelism" in *Substance of Faith,* 35.

36. Ibid., 37.

37. Clarence Jordan, Koinonia Partners tape collection, # KR 2076, "The Man from Gadera," (Americus, Ga.: Koinonia Records, n.d.). See also Clarence Jordan, "Incarnational Evangelism" in *Substance of Faith,* 34-7.

38. Jordan, "Incarnational Evangelism" in *Substance of Faith,* 18.

39. Ibid.

40. Jordan, "The Adventures of Three Students in a Fiery Furnace" in *Substance of Faith,* 47.

41. Jordan, "Incarnational Evangelism" in *Substance of Faith,* 18.

42. Jordan, "The Adventures of Three Students in a Fiery Furnace" in *Substance of Faith,* 46-47.

43. Ibid., 46.

44. Ibid.

45. Ibid., 46-54.

46. James McClendon, *Biography as Theology: How Life Stories Can Remake Today's Theology* (Nashville, Tenn.: Abingdon Press, 1974), 112, *McClendon's italics.*

47. Jordan, "Incarnational Evangelism" in *Substance of Faith,* 31-8.

48. Jordan, "The Father's Pursuing Love" *in Substance of Faith,* 148-51.

49. McClendon, *Biography as Theology,* 112.

Chapter 8

1. Tracy Elaine K'Meyer, *Interracialism and Christian Community in the Postwar South: The Story of Koinonia Farm* (Charlottesville, Va.: University Press of Virginia, 1997), 128.

2. Ibid.

3. Ibid.

4. Ibid., 127.

5. Ibid., 128-9.

6. Ibid., 129.

7. Ibid., 130.

8. Ibid., 128-9.

9. "White Children Barred from Georgia School," *The Christian Century* 77 (Oct. 5, 1960): 1140. On the same page, the reporter commented, "It seems a pity that opposition to the principles held by adult Koinonians has to take itself out on children, no matter what their color. But then, isn't the whole program of opposition to abolition of segregation in education an attack on children?"

10. "Court Orders Americus High to Admit Koinonia Students," *The Macon Telegraph* (Oct. 26, 1960): 1.

11. Clarence Jordan, "The Christian, War, Violence, and Nonviolence," in Henlee H. Barnette, *Clarence Jordan: Turning Dreams into Deeds* (Macon, Ga.: Smyth & Helwys Publishing, 1992), 30.

12. Ibid.

13. Ibid., 31-2.

14. Ibid., 32.

15. Ibid., 33.

16. Ibid.

17. Ibid., 34.

18. Clarence Jordan, "Incarnational Evangelism," in *The Substance of Faith and Other Cotton Patch Sermons*, ed. Dallas Lee (New York: Association Press, 1972), 43.

19. Ibid.

20. Ibid., 44.

21. Ibid., 45.

22. Clarence Jordan Papers, Hargrett Rare Book and Manuscript Library at the University of Georgia Libraries, Athens, Ga., Manuscript #756, Box 2, Folder 14.

23. Ron E. Roberts, *The New Communes: Coming Together in America* (Englewood Cliffs, N.J.: Prentice-Hall, 1971), 66.

24. Dallas Lee, *The Cotton Patch Evidence: The Story of Clarence Jordan and the Koinonia Farm Experiment (1942-1970)* (New York: Harper & Row, 1971), 175-6.

25. Although Reba Place members thought they were creating something new, their community was extremely similar in form to the Catholic Worker houses that had been begun in the 1930s.

26. Lee, *Cotton Patch Evidence*, 176.

27. Clarence Jordan Papers, Box 6, Folder 1, March 28, 1960, letter from Clarence Jordan to Reba Place Fellowship.

28. Clarence Jordan Papers, #756, Box 6, Folder 2, n.d., conference report.

29. For example, Michael Westmoreland-White, "Incarnational Discipleship: The Ethics of Clarence Jordan, Martin Luther King Jr., and Dorothy Day," unpublished dissertation, Southern Baptist Theological Seminary, May 1995.

30. Jordan did not mention Gandhi or Martin Luther King Jr. in his writings or sermons, and none of Gandhi's writings were found in Jordan's library. He would have been familiar with their ideas in general through the news and discussions at Koinonia Farm.

31. K'Meyer, *Interracialism,* 95.

32. Ibid.

33. Ibid., 110-1.

34. Ibid., 111.

35. Taylor Branch, *Parting the Waters: America in the King Years, 1954-1963* (New York: Simon & Schuster, 1988), 864-5.

36. K'Meyer, *Interracialism,* 137.

37. Jan Jordan Zehr, in *Koinonia Remembered: The First Fifty Years,* ed. Kay Weiner (Americus, Ga.: Koinonia Partners, 1992), 77.

38. Ibid., 77-8.

39. Ibid., 78.

40. Ibid.

41. K'Meyer, *Interracialism,* 137.

42. Ibid., 135.

43. Ibid.

44. Ibid.

45. Clarence Jordan Papers, #756, Box 6, Folder 3, March 13, 1961, newsletter from Dorothy Swisshelm to Brothers and Sisters in Christ. See also K'Meyer, *Interracialism,* 133-5.

46. Koinonia Farm Newsletters, Vertical File, University of Georgia, Athens, Ga.

47. Paul Harvey, *Redeeming the South: Religious Cultures and Racial Identities Among Southern Baptists 1865-1925* (Chapel Hill, N.C.: The University of North Carolina Press, 1997), 1-13.

48. K'Meyer, *Interracialism,* 96.

49. Ibid., 97.

50. Ibid.

51. Ibid.

52. Ibid., 129.

53. Clarence Jordan Papers, #756, Box 6, Folder 3, Koinonia Farm Newsletter, December 21, 1958.

54. Lee, *Cotton Patch Evidence,* 59.

55. Ibid., 60.

56. Ibid., 61.

57. K'Meyer, *Interracialism*, 179-80.

58. Jimmy Carter, *Living Faith* (New York: Random House, 1996), 49, 51.

59. Ibid., 53-4.

60. Ibid., 62-5.

61. Ibid., 68-9.

62. Jimmy Carter, *Turning Point* (New York: Random House, 1992), 21.

63. Ibid.

64. K'Meyer, *Interracialism*, 134.

65. Carter, *Living Faith*, 6.

66. Ibid., 7.

67. Lee, *Cotton Patch Evidence*, 197-203.

68. Millard Fuller, "Building the Kingdom of God," in *Kingdom Building: Essays from the Grassroots of Habitat*, eds. David Johnson Rowe and Robert William Stevens (Americus, Ga.: Habitat for Humanity, 1984), 17.

69. Millard Fuller, *Bokotola* (Clinton, N.J.: New Win Publishing, 1977), 16-20, *Jordan's italics*.

Chapter 9

1. Clarence Jordan Papers, Hargrett Rare Book and Manuscript Library at the University of Georgia Libraries, Athens, Ga., Manuscript #756, box 3, Folder 3, May 16, 1955, letter from Russ Berry to Clarence Jordan.

2. Clarence Jordan Papers, #756, Box 6, Folder 1, May 13, 1960, letter from James S. Best to Clarence Jordan.

3. Clarence Jordan, *The Cotton Patch Version of Hebrews and the General Epistles* (Clinton, N.J.: New Win Publishing, 1970), 6. The Cotton Patch version of Hebrews was first copyrighted in 1963 and James in 1964.

4. Hebrews 12:1-2 and James 2:26.

5. Jordan, *Hebrews and the General Epistles*, 15.

6. Ibid.

7. Ibid.

8. Ibid., 28-30.

9. Ibid., 38-9.

10. Ibid., 49.

11. Ibid., 35.

12.   Henlee H. Barnette, *Clarence Jordan: Turning Dreams into Deeds* (Macon, Ga.: Smyth & Helwys Publishing, 1992).

13.   Clarence Jordan, *The Cotton Patch Version of Paul's Epistles* (Clinton, N.J.: New Win Publishing, 1968), 7-11.

14.   Ibid., 7.

15.   Ibid.

16.   Ibid.

17.   Ibid., 11 for a discussion of Pauline authorship.

18.   Ibid., 8.

19.   Ibid., 9.

20.   Ibid., 8.

21.   Ibid., 8-9.

22.   Ibid., 9.

23.   Ibid.

24.   Ibid., 31, *Jordan's italics*. In his footnote to this text, Jordan mentions that he is not trying to single out Protestants, but he uses them because the South had many Protestants and his audience was primarily Protestant. He does not issue a similar disclaimer regarding the white people.

25.   Ibid., 32, *Jordan's italics*.

26.   Ibid., footnote 15.

27.   Ibid., 36.

28.   Ibid., 99 and 108.

29.   Ibid., 99, *Jordan's italics*.

30.   Ibid., 108.

31.   Jordan, *The Cotton Patch Version of Luke and Acts: Jesus' Doings and the Happenings"* (Clinton, N.J.: New Win Publishing, 1969).

32.   Ibid., 112, Acts 9:28-29.

33.   Ibid., 114, Acts 10:9-16.

34.   Ibid., 115-6, *Jordan's italics*; Acts 10:28-29 and 34-36.

35.   Ibid., 134, Acts 18:2-4.

36.   Ibid., 25, *Jordan's italics*.

37.   Jordan, *Luke and Acts,* 47, footnote 7.

38.   Jordan, *Luke and Acts,* 47, footnote 8.

39.   Jordan, *Luke and Acts,* 47, footnote 9.

40.   Clarence Jordan, *Luke and Acts,* 46-7, Luke 10:25-37, *Jordan's italics*.

41.   Ibid., 61, Luke 15:1-2, *Jordan's italics*.

42.   Clarence Jordan, *The Cotton Patch Version of Matthew and John* (Clinton, N.J.: New Win Publishing, 1970), 18, and Jordan, *Luke and Acts,* 21.

43. Jordan, *Matthew and John,* 16-7; and Jordan, *Luke and Acts,* 18-20.

44. Jordan, *Luke and Acts,* 95-6.

45. Jordan, *Paul's Epistles,* 37.

46. Ibid., 33.

47. For example, see Jordan, *Luke and Acts,* 44 and 91.

48. Ray F. Martens, Review of *The Cotton Patch Version of Paul's Epistles,* in *The Springfielder* 32:1 (Spring 1968): 46.

49. Ibid.

50. Louis Martyn, Review of *The Cotton Patch Version of Luke and Acts* in *Union Seminary Quarterly Review* 25 (Fall 1969): 382.

51. Martens, Review of *Paul's Epistles,* 47.

52. Martyn, Review of *Luke and Acts,* 383.

53. Jordan, *Matthew and John,* 31, Matthew 7:28-9, *Jordan's italics.*

Chapter 10

1. Dallas Lee, *The Cotton Patch Evidence: The Story of Clarence Jordan and the Koinonia Farm Experiment (1942-1970)* (New York: Harper & Row, 1971), 230.

2. Ibid., 232.

3. Linda Fuller, in *Koinonia Remembered: The First Fifty Years,* ed. Kay Weiner (Americus, Ga.: Koinonia Partners, 1992), 104.

4. Lee, *Cotton Patch Evidence,* 233.

5. Linda Fuller, in *Koinonia Remembered,* ed. Weiner, 106.

6. Ibid.

7. Lee, *Cotton Patch Evidence,* 233.

8. Millard Fuller, *Bokotola,* (Clinton, N.J.: New Win Publishing, 1977), 22.

9. Ibid.

10. Ibid., 23; Clarence Jordan, *The Cotton Patch Version of Hebrews and the General Epistles* (Clinton, N.J.: New Win Publishing, 1970), 58; see 1 Peter 1:24-5.

11. Fuller, *Bokotola,* 23.

12. Le Roy J. Day, "Koinonia Partners: An Intentional Community Since 1942," *Communal Societies* 10 (1990): 118.

13. Ibid.

14. Rosabeth Moss Kanter, *Commitment and Community: Communes and Utopias in Sociological Perspective* (Cambridge: Harvard University Press, 1972), 157-61.

15. David Janzen, *Fire, Salt, and Peace: Intentional Christian Communities Alive in North America* (Evanston, Ill.: Paralepsis Books, 1996), 106-8.

16. Day, "Koinonia Partners," 123; also Janzen, *Fire, Salt, and Peace,* 106.

17. Day, 123.

18. Donald E. Pitzer, ed., *America's Communal Utopias* (Chapel Hill, N.C.: University of North Carolina Press, 1999), 474.

19. Day, "Koinonia Partners," 117.

20. Fuller, *Bokotola,* 24.

21. See Fuller, *Bokotola,* for a complete history of the beginning of Habitat for Humanity.

22. Clyde Tilley, "Habitat for Humanity: A Holistic Ministry" in *Kingdom Building: Essays from the Grassroots of Habitat,* eds. David Johnson Rowe and Robert William Stevens (Americus, Ga.: Habitat for Humanity, 1984), 34.

23. Tom Key and Russell Treyz, *Cotton Patch Gospel,* videocassette (Americus, Ga.: Koinonia Partners, 1988).

24. Kanter, *Commitment and Community,* 192-236.

25. Ibid., 157-61.

26. Ibid., 246-8.

27. Ibid., 192-3.

28. Ibid., 214.

Bibliography of Clarence Jordan's Works

A. Books

Jordan, Clarence. *The Cotton Patch Version of Hebrews and General Epistles*. Clinton, N.J.: New Win Publishing, Inc., 1970.

_____. *The Cotton Patch Version of Luke and Acts: Jesus' Doings and the Happenings*. Clinton, N.J.: New Win Publishing, Inc., 1969.

_____. *The Cotton Patch Version of Matthew and John*. Clinton, N.J.: New Win Publishing, Inc., 1970.

_____. *The Cotton Patch Version of Paul's Epistles*. Clinton, N.J.: New Win Publishing, Inc., 1968.

_____. "Jesus and Possessions." In *Kingdom Building: Essays from the Grassroots of Habitat*. Robert William Stevens and David Johnson Rowe, eds. Americus, Ga.: Habitat for Humanity, Inc., 1984.

_____. *Sermon on the Mount*. Valley Forge, Pa.: Judson Press, 1952.

_____. "A Spirit of Partnership." In *Kingdom Building: Essays from the Grassroots of Habitat*. Robert William Stevens and David Johnson Rowe, eds. Americus, Ga.: Habitat for Humanity, Inc., 1984.

_____. *The Substance of Faith and Other Cotton Patch Sermons by Clarence Jordan*. Dallas Lee, ed. New York: Association Press, 1972.

_____. *Why Study the Bible?* Philadelphia: Baptist Youth Fellowship, 1953.

Jordan, Clarence, and Bill Lane Doulos. *Cotton Patch Parables of Liberation*. Scottdale, Pa.: Herald Press, 1976.

B. Dissertation
Jordan, Clarence. "The Meaning of *Thanatos and Nekros* in the Epistles of Paul." Unpublished doctoral dissertation. Southern Baptist Theological Seminary, Louisville, Ky., 1938.

C. Periodicals
Jordan, Clarence. "*As You Want People to Act Toward You.*" *The Church Advocate* (September 1967): 8-9.

_____. "Christian Community in the South." *Journal of Religious Thought* 14 (Autumn-Winter 1956-57): 27-36.

_____. "Dr. Jordan's Statement." *The Longrunner* (August 1942): 2.

_____. "The Good Samaritan." *Mennonite Life* (January 1967): 17-8.

_____. "Impractical Christianity." *Sunday School Young Peoples' Quarterly* (Third Quarter 1948): 2.

_____. "In the Land of Great Violence." *The Mennonite* 25 (May 1965): 353.

_____. "Is It an Impossible Job?" *Young People* 12 (August 1956): 9-10.

_____. "Is Non-Violence Enough?" *Baptist Leader* (February 1964): 12-3.

_____. "Learn to Take It on the Chin." *The Church Advocate* (August 1966): 8-9.

_____. "Love Your Enemies." *Post American* 2 (May-June 1973): 4-5.

_____. "The Meaning of Christian Fellowship." *Prophetic Religion* 7 (Spring 1946): 3-6.

_____. "One Jesus for Another." *Christian Living* (October 1965): 20-2.

_____. "A Parable of No Violence, Some Violence, and Great Violence." *Town and Country Church* (November-December 1965): 9.

_____. "A Personal Letter to Friends of Koinonia Farm." *The Church Advocate* (July 1969): 12-3."

_____. "Racial Frontiers." *Baptist Student* (November 1941): 6-7.

_____. "The Rich Farmer." *The Presbyterian Outlook* (March 27, 1967): 4.

_____. "The Sound of a Dove." *Town and Country Church* (1961): 16.

_____. "When Jesus Came to Georgia." *The Church Advocate* (February 1967): 8-9.

Index

About the Author

Raised in Alabama, Ann Louise Coble teaches Christian education and religion at Westminster College in New Wilmington, Pennsylvania. Coble did her master's work at Covenant Seminary (St. Louis, Mo.) and Gordon-Conwell Seminary (South Hamilton, Mass.) She received her Ph.D. from St. Louis University.